Great Meals in Minutes

Family Menus

Great Meals in Minutes was created by Rebus Inc., and published by Time-Life Books.

This edition published 1995 by Bloomsbury Books, an imprint of The Godfrey Cave Group, 42 Bloomsbury Street, London, WC1B 3QJ.

© 1995 Time-Life Books BV.

ISBN 1 85471 533 X

Printed and bound in Great Britain.

Family Menus

Bloomsbury Books
London

Diana Sturgis

Menu 1
(Left)
Risi e Bisi Soup
Individual Sausage and Cheese Pizzas
Sliced Oranges and Kiwis

Diana Sturgis grew up in a rural area of South Wales where, she says, 'fresh foods and sophisticated ingredients were hard to come by.' Today, the meals she prepares for her own family are very different from those she ate as a child. She takes advantage of the abundance of fresh produce and imported ingredients widely available in this country, cooking foods that her children already like as well as dishes that are new to the family.

The three menus she offers here are all Italian-style and easy to make. Menu 1 features individual sausage and cheese pizzas, which are preceded by a soup of rice and peas (*risi e bisi*), slivered ham, and chopped spinach. Orange and kiwi fruit slices are the colourful dessert.

In Menu 2, the stuffed peppers are nearly a meal in themselves, with their rich filling of Italian sausage, bread crumbs, cheese, and pine nuts. Toasted garlic bread and a salad of tomatoes with red onion and fresh basil go well with the peppers.

Diana Sturgis finds that pasta is always a winner at the family table. In Menu 3, she serves a hearty casserole of baked ziti (hollow tubular pasta) with tomato sauce, meatballs, and three types of cheese. Spinach with mushrooms, scallions, and homemade croutons is the simple salad.

For this informal family dinner, offer the soup before the main course of small pizzas topped with tomato sauce, cheese, and a mosaic of sausage slices. The orange and kiwi dessert is enhanced by a dollop of sour cream and a sprinkling of brown sugar.

**Risi e Bisi Soup
Individual Sausage and Cheese Pizzas
Sliced Oranges and Kiwis**

Each single-serving pizza is topped with slices of sweet sausage, a staple of Italian cookery. Italian sweet sausages, available in links at most supermarkets, are usually seasoned with garlic, fennel seeds, and ground black pepper.

Kiwi fruit, named for the fuzzy New Zealand bird it resembles, is a rich source of vitamin C. Brown-skinned with lime-green flesh and tiny edible seeds, this tart-sweet fruit is a natural partner for oranges. To ripen hard kiwis, leave them in a closed paper bag with a ripe apple or banana for a couple of days at room temperature. California kiwis are sold from October to May; those imported from New Zealand may be purchased in the summer.

Start-to-Finish Steps
1   Follow fruit recipe steps 1 to 4.
2   Follow pizzas recipe step 1 and soup recipe step 1.
3   Follow pizzas recipe steps 2 to 5.
4   While sausages are simmering, follow soup recipe steps 2 to 5.
5   While rice is cooking, follow pizzas recipe steps 6 to 10.
6   Follow soup recipe steps 6 to 9.
7   Follow pizzas recipe steps 11 to 13.

8   While pizzas are baking, follow soup recipe step 10 and serve as first course.
9   Follow pizzas recipe step 14 and serve as main course.
10 Follow fruit recipe step 5 and serve for dessert.

Risi e Bisi Soup

250 g (^{1}/$_{2}$lb) fresh spinach, or 300 g (10 oz) package frozen chopped spinach
60 g (2 oz) long-grain rice
300 g (10 oz) package frozen tiny green peas
60 g (2 oz) thinly sliced good-quality baked ham (about 2 or 3 slices)
750 ml (1^{1}/$_{2}$ pts) chicken stock

1   Wash fresh spinach, if using, in several changes of cold water to remove grit. Remove and discard tough stems; set spinach aside.
2   Bring 60 ml (2 fl oz) water to a rapid boil in medium-size saucepan over high heat. Add fresh spinach to boiling water, cover pan, and cook 2 minutes.
3   Meanwhile, combine rice with 250 ml (^{1}/$_{2}$ pt) of water in small saucepan and bring to a boil over medium-high heat. Reduce heat, cover, and simmer gently 16 to 17 minutes, or just until rice is tender and water is absorbed.
4   Turn spinach into large strainer and drain, pressing with back of spoon to eliminate excess moisture. Coarsely chop spinach; set aside. Rinse pan; set aside. If using frozen spinach, cut package in half with chef's knife or cleaver. Place one half in freezer bag and return to freezer; set remaining half aside. Repeat for frozen peas.
5   Stack ham slices and cut into thin slices; set aside.
6   When rice is done, remove from heat and fluff with fork; cover pan and set aside.
7   In medium-size saucepan, combine half of the stock, the frozen spinach, if using, and peas, and bring to a boil over medium heat. Reduce heat to low and simmer very gently about 4 minutes, or until spinach is thawed and peas are tender.
8   Meanwhile, transfer half the rice to blender or food processor fitted with steel blade. Add remaining stock and process 1 minute, or until puréed.

9   Add puréed rice, remaining boiled rice, slivered ham, and fresh cooked spinach, if using, to stock mixture in saucepan and stir to combine; cover pan and set aside.

10 When ready to serve, reheat soup briefly over medium heat and divide among 4 bowls.

Individual Sausage and Cheese Pizzas

1 packet 7.5 g ($^1/_4$ oz) fast-acting yeast
1 level tablespoon granulated sugar
2 tablespoons vegetable oil, approximately
350 g (12 oz) flour, preferably bread flour or unbleached plain flour, approximately
1 teaspoon salt
3 tablespoons olive oil
2 to 3 sweet Italian sausages (about 250 g ($^1/_2$ lb) total weight)
250 g (8 oz) package mozzarella cheese
2 level tablespoons yellow cornmeal, approximately
250 g (8 oz) can tomato sauce
1 teaspoon dried oregano

1   For pizza dough, combine yeast and sugar in small bowl. Add 250 ml ($^1/_2$ pt) warm (110 degrees) tap water, stir to combine, and set aside 5 minutes, or until mixture foams.

2   Lightly grease medium-size bowl with vegetable oil; set aside.

3   Combine flour and salt in bowl of food processor fitted with dough blade. With processor running, slowly add 2 tablespoons olive oil, then add yeast mixture. Dough will quickly form a ball on top of blade (this takes 20 to 30 seconds). If dough is too moist to form a ball, add a bit more flour and process another few seconds, until dough is smooth and elastic. Or, combine ingredients in a second medium-size bowl and stir with wooden spoon until dough is smooth and elastic.

4   Turn dough into greased bowl, cover with kitchen towel, and set aside to rise in warm place for 20 minutes.

5   Meanwhile, prick sausages in several places with fork and place in small skillet. Add enough cold water to cover and bring to a boil over high heat. Reduce heat and simmer sausages, uncovered, 15 minutes.

6   Drain sausages and set aside to cool.

7   Using food processor fitted with shredding disc, or coarse side of grater, shred mozzarella; set aside.

8   Cut sausages crosswise into 5 mm ($^1/_4$ inch) thick slices; set aside.

9   Arrange 2 racks approximately 7$^1/_2$ cm (3 inches) apart in middle of oven and preheat oven to 230°C (450°F or Mark 8).

10 Rub four 20 or 23 cm (8 or 9 inch) metal pie pans, two 27 by 43 cm (11 by 17 inch) heavy-gauge cookie sheets, or a combination of both, with vegetable oil; set aside.

11 Turn dough out onto work surface and knead briefly. Divide into 4 equal portions and shape each into a smooth ball.

12 Lightly sprinkle work surface with cornmeal to prevent dough from sticking. Press and roll out each ball of dough into 20 cm (8 inch) round and place each round in prepared pie pan, or place 2 rounds on each cookie sheet.

13 Brush a 2$^1/_2$ cm (1 inch) border of remaining olive oil around edge of each pizza. Pour 4 tablespoons of tomato sauce onto each pizza and spread evenly with back of spoon, leaving a 1 cm ($^1/_2$ inch) border free of sauce. Sprinkle each pizza with mozzarella and $^1/_4$ teaspoon oregano. Divide sausage among pizzas and bake 12 to 15 minutes, switching pans on shelves after 5 minutes to prevent the lower pizzas from burning.

14 To serve, cut each pizza into 6 wedges with a pizza wheel or chef's knife, or serve whole.

Sliced Oranges and Kiwis

3 navel oranges
3 kiwi fruits
60 ml (2 fl oz) sour cream
1 level tablespoon dark brown sugar

1   With sharp paring knife, cut 5 mm ($^1/_4$ inch) thick slice from stem end and base of each orange. Place orange firmly on plate and, using a downward sawing motion, cut away peel and as much white pith as possible, turning the fruit as you trim off each strip. Repeat for remaining oranges; discard peel.

2   Cut each orange crosswise into 5 mm ($^1/_4$ inch) thick rounds; set aside.

3   Using paring knife, remove peel from kiwis and discard. Cut kiwis crosswise into 5 mm ($^1/_4$ inch) thick rounds; set aside.

4   Divide orange and kiwi slices among 4 dessert plates, arranging them in a decorative pattern. Cover with plastic wrap and refrigerate until ready to serve.

5   Just before serving, top each dessert with a dollop of sour cream and sprinkle with brown sugar.

Italian-style Stuffed Peppers
Marinated Tomato and Red Onion Salad
Garlic Bread

Stuffed bell peppers, marinated tomato and red onion salad, and crusty garlic bread are an easy Italian meal.

Thick-skinned peppers are best for stuffing; choose those with relatively even bottoms so they do not topple over during baking. Look for peppers that are firm and shiny, with no signs of decay. They should feel hefty for their size. Be sure to remove all of the seeds before cooking because they are often bitter.

Start-to-Finish Steps

1 Peel and mince enough yellow onion to measure 60 g (2 oz) for peppers recipe. For salad recipe, peel and cut 4 thin slices crosswise from red onion and separate into rings; mince enough remaining red onion to measure 2 tablespoons. Wash parsley, and fresh basil if using, and pat dry with paper towels. Trim stems from parsley and discard. Finely chop enough parsley to measure 15 g ($^1/_2$ oz) for peppers recipe. Strip 12 basil leaves from stems. Coarsely chop 8 leaves for salad recipe and set aside 4 leaves for garnish. Reserve remaining herbs for another use.
2 Follow peppers recipe steps 1 to 8.
3 While peppers are baking, follow salad recipe steps 1 to 5.
4 Follow peppers recipe step 9.
5 While peppers finish baking, follow garlic bread recipe steps 1 to 4.
6 Follow peppers recipe step 10, turn on grill, and follow garlic bread recipe step 5.
7 Follow salad recipe step 6, peppers recipe step 11, garlic bread recipe step 6, and serve.

Italian-style Stuffed Peppers

4 to 5 sweet Italian sausages (about 500 g (1 lb) total weight)
60 g (2 oz) Parmesan cheese
2 slices firm home-style white bread
60 g (2 oz) minced yellow onion
15 g ($^1/_2$ oz) finely chopped fresh parsley
3 level tablespoons pine nuts
$^1/_2$ teaspoon dried oregano
Pinch of freshly ground black pepper
4 medium-size green bell peppers (about 750 g (1$^1/_2$ lb) total weight)
2 tablespoons olive oil, preferably fruity extra-virgin

1 Preheat oven to 180°C (350°F or Mark 4).
2 Remove and discard sausage casings. Crumble sausage meat and place in large bowl.
3 In food processor fitted with steel blade, or with grater, grate Parmesan. Add half of Parmesan to bowl with sausage; set remainder aside.
4 Trim crusts from bread and discard. Using food processor, or coarse side of grater, grate enough bread to measure 60 g (2 oz) plus 2 tablespoons crumbs. Add 60 g (2 oz) crumbs to bowl with sausage and cheese; set remainder aside.
5 Add onion, parsley, pine nuts, oregano, and black pepper to sausage mixture and stir to combine.
6 Wash peppers and dry with paper towels. Cut 1 cm ($^1/_2$ inch) thick slice from top of each pepper; remove and discard seeds. Mince edible parts of tops and add them to stuffing mixture.
7 Place peppers in 23 by 23 cm (9 by 9 inch) shallow baking dish. Divide stuffing among peppers, mounding it slightly if necessary, and drizzle with oil. Bake peppers 35 minutes.
8 Meanwhile, in small bowl, combine remaining 30 g (1 oz) Parmesan and 2 tablespoons bread crumbs; set aside.
9 Increase oven temperature to 190°C (375°F or Mark 5), sprinkle peppers with Parmesan mixture, and bake another 10 minutes.
10 Remove peppers from oven, cover loosely with foil, and keep warm on stove top until ready to serve.
11 When ready to serve, using metal spatula, divide peppers among dinner plates.

Marinated Tomato and Red Onion Salad

500 g (1 lb) Italian plum tomatoes or other flavourful ripe tomatoes
4 tablespoons olive oil, preferably fruity extra-virgin
1 tablespoon red wine vinegar
$^1/_2$ teaspoon salt
Pinch of sugar
Pinch of dry mustard
2 level tablespoons minced red onion plus 4 thin slices, separated into rings
8 fresh basil leaves, coarsely chopped, plus 4 leaves for garnish, or $^1/_4$ teaspoon dried basil
$^1/_4$ teaspoon freshly ground black pepper

1 Bring 1$^1/_4$ ltrs (2 pts) of water to a boil in medium-size saucepan over high heat.
2 With paring knife, make small incision in base of each tomato. Plunge tomatoes into boiling water for 15 seconds. With slotted spoon, transfer tomatoes to colander and refresh under cold running water.
3 Meanwhile, in small non-aluminum bowl, combine oil, vinegar, salt, sugar, and dry mustard, and whisk until blended; set aside.

11

4 When tomatoes are cool enough to handle, remove skins and discard. Cut tomatoes crosswise into 1 cm (1/2 inch) thick slices and arrange half of them in a single layer in shallow glass or ceramic dish. Sprinkle with half of the minced red onion, basil, and pepper. Top with remaining tomato slices and sprinkle with remaining minced onion, basil, and pepper. Top tomatoes with onion rings.
5 Whisk dressing to recombine and pour over salad. Set aside to marinate at least 15 minutes at room temperature.
6 Using slotted spoon, divide salad among 4 dinner plates and garnish each serving with a basil leaf.

Garlic Bread

1 loaf Italian bread
2 cloves garlic
125 ml (4 fl oz) olive oil, preferably fruity extra-virgin
Salt
Freshly ground black pepper

1 Halve bread lengthwise; set aside.
2 Crush garlic under flat blade of chef's knife. Remove peels and discard.
3 Rub cut surfaces of bread with crushed garlic; reserve garlic.
4 In small skillet, combine olive oil and garlic, and warm over low heat about 5 minutes.
5 Remove garlic from oil and discard. Brush cut surfaces of bread liberally with warm oil, sprinkle with salt and pepper to taste, and arrange bread, cut-side-up, on baking sheet. Place bread in preheated grill 10 cm (4 inches) from heating element and toast 2 to 3 minutes, or until golden brown and crisp.
6 Remove bread from grill. Cut on diagonal into 5 cm (2 inch) wide pieces and divide among dinner plates or serve in napkin-lined basket.

Added touch
This refreshing iced dessert – perfect for a hot summer evening – retains the flavour of fresh watermelon. If watermelon is out of season, substitute 1 1/4 ltrs (2 pts) of apple juice, and proceed with the recipe.

Watermelon Ice

2.5 Kg (5 lb) ripe watermelon
1 tablespoon freshly squeezed lemon juice
125 g (4 oz) sugar, approximately

1 Using chef's knife, cut pulp from watermelon rind and place in large bowl; discard rind. Mash pulp with potato masher until completely broken down. In batches, force mashed pulp through sieve set over medium-size bowl, pressing with back of spoon. Or, beat pulp with electric mixer and then sieve. You should have about 1 1/4 ltrs (2 pts) juice.
2 Add lemon juice and sugar to taste to watermelon juice, and stir until sugar is dissolved.
3 Pour fruit syrup into ice-cream machine and freeze according to manufacturer's instructions. Or, pour into 2 metal ice-cube trays and freeze about 1 hour, or until mushy. Pour into food processor or blender and turn machine on and off 2 or 3 times to break up ice crystals. Return to ice-cube trays and refreeze. Repeat, if necessary, to achieve desired texture.
4 Divide ice among 4 bowls or goblets and serve.

**Baked Ziti
Spinach salad with Mushrooms and
Homemade Croutons**

Let everyone help themselves to baked ziti casserole and crisp spinach salad with mushrooms and croutons.

13

The ziti casserole combines some favourite children's foods – meatballs, pasta, and mild cheeses. This recipe will please busy parents, too. You can prepare the dish early in the day and cover and refrigerate it until baking time.

The accompanying iron-rich spinach salad with buttery croutons will also appeal to youngsters. If possible, buy loose spinach rather than the packed type, which often contains many damaged leaves. Spinach should have a fresh odour; if there is any trace of a sour smell, do not buy it. The leaves should be fresh and dark green without wilt or bruises. Unwashed spinach can be refrigerated for up to 5 days, but it is best used as soon as possible. Before serving, rinse the spinach thoroughly. To stem the leaves, fold each in half lengthwise with the underside facing out, then pull off the stem.

Start-to-Finish Steps

1. Follow ziti recipe steps 1 to 7.
2. While meatballs simmer, follow salad recipe steps 1 and 2.
3. Follow ziti recipe steps 8 to 13.
4. While ziti is baking, follow salad recipe steps 3 to 11.
5. Follow ziti recipe step 14 and serve with salad.

Baked Ziti

Small yellow onion
Small bunch parsley
2 tablespoons olive oil
60 g (2 oz) Parmesan cheese
850 g (1 3/4 lb) can Italian plum tomatoes in purée
4 tablespoons tomato paste
1 bay leaf
1/2 teaspoon dried oregano
1/2 teaspoon dried basil
Pinch of sugar
2 teaspoons salt
1/4 teaspoon freshly ground black pepper
350 g (3/4 lb) lean minced beef
45 g (1 1/2 oz) dry breadcrumbs
1 egg
250 g (8 oz) package mozzarella cheese
350 g (3/4 lb) ziti
250 g (8 oz) whole-milk ricotta cheese

1. Halve and peel onion. Chop enough to measure 100 g (3 oz); set aside.
2. Wash parsley and dry with paper towels. Trim stems and discard. Chop enough parsley to measure 30 g (1 oz); set aside.
3. Heat olive oil in medium-size heavy-gauge non-aluminium saucepan or casserole over medium heat. Add chopped onion and sauté, stirring occasionally, 2 minutes, or until softened but not browned.
4. Meanwhile, grate enough Parmesan in food processor or with grater to measure 60 g (2 oz) ; set aside.
5. Add tomatoes with purée to pan and stir, crushing tomatoes with edge of spoon or potato masher. Stir in tomato paste, bay leaf, oregano, basil, sugar, 1/2 teaspoon salt, and 1/8 teaspoon pepper, and bring to a gentle boil.
6. Crumble minced meat into large bowl. Add two thirds of the parsley, bread crumbs, grated Parmesan, 1/2 teaspoon salt, and remaining 1/8 teaspoon pepper. Add egg and stir with fork until mixture is well combined. With wet hands, shape mixture into 2 1/2 cm (1 inch) meatballs. You will have about 30 meatballs.
7. Stir sauce to be sure it is not sticking to bottom of pan. Drop meatballs into boiling sauce and simmer gently, uncovered, turning meatballs occasionally but not stirring, 20 minutes.
8. Preheat oven to 190°C (375°F or Mark 5).
9. Bring 3 1/2 ltrs (6 pts) of water and 1 teaspoon salt to a boil in stockpot or large saucepan.
10. While water is heating, shred mozzarella in food processor fitted with shredding disk, or with grater, set aside.
11. Stir ziti into boiling water and cook about 9 minutes, or just until *al dente*. Do *not* overcook.
12. Turn ziti into colander and drain well.
13. Remove bay leaf from sauce and discard. Spoon off any fat from the surface before proceeding. Turn half of the tomato sauce and meatballs into 32 by 23 by 5 cm (13 by 9 by 2 inch) baking pan.

Spread ziti over sauce. Top ziti with mozzarella and remaining sauce and meatballs. Dot with spoonfuls of ricotta cheese and bake 20 minutes, or until piping hot.

14 Sprinkle baked ziti with remaining parsley and serve from baking pan.

Spinach Salad with Mushrooms and Homemade Croutons

500 g (1 lb) fresh spinach
Small bunch scallions
1 clove garlic
1 loaf Italian bread, preferably stale
4 level tablespoons unsalted butter
350 g (3/4 lb) mushrooms
1 lemon
1/4 teaspoon salt
Pinch of freshly ground black pepper

1 Wash spinach thoroughly in several changes of cold water. Dry in salad spinner or with paper towels. Remove and discard any bruised or discoloured leaves. Remove tough stems and discard. Tear spinach leaves into bite-size pieces and place in large salad bowl.

2 Wash scallions and dry with paper towels. Trim ends and discard. Cut enough scallions crosswise into 5 mm (1/4 inch) pieces to measure 60 g (2 oz). Add sliced scallions to bowl with spinach, cover with plastic wrap, and refrigerate until ready to serve. Reserve remaining scallions for another use.

3 Crush garlic under flat blade of chef's knife. Remove peel and discard. Set garlic aside.

4 Cut enough bread into 1 cm (1/2 inch) cubes to measure 100 g (3 oz); reserve remainder for another use.

5 Combine garlic and 2 tablespoons butter in medium-size skillet or sauté pan over medium heat. When foaming subsides, remove and discard garlic. Add bread cubes and sauté, stirring occasionally, about 5 minutes, or until crisp and golden.

6 Meanwhile, wipe mushrooms clean with damp paper towels. Cut mushrooms into 2 1/2 cm (1/8 inch) thick slices; set aside.

7 With slotted spoon, transfer croutons to paper-towel-lined plate; set aside.

8 Add remaining butter to skillet and melt over medium heat. When foaming subsides, add mushrooms and sauté, stirring occasionally, about 7 minutes, or until the liquid they yield has evaporated and mushrooms are beginning to brown at the edges.

9 Remove pan from heat and set aside.

10 Squeeze enough lemon juice to measure 2 tablespoons.

11 Add lemon juice, salt, and pepper to spinach and scallions, and toss to combine. Add croutons and mushrooms, and toss.

Added touch
Tortoni is an Italian ice-cream with a mousse-like consistency. Here, the cook adds gingersnap crumbs to the mixture for extra flavour.

Gingersnap Tortoni

Seven 5 cm (2 inch) gingersnaps
1 egg
60 g (2 oz) caster sugar
250 ml (8 fl oz) heavy cream, well chilled
1/2 teaspoon vanilla extract
2 level tablespoons blanched slivered almonds

1 Place gingersnaps between 2 sheets of waxed paper and crush with rolling pin. Measure out 60 g (2 oz) crumbs and set aside.

2 Separate egg, placing white in medium-size bowl and reserving yolk for another use. With electric mixer at high speed, beat egg white until soft peaks form. Add one quarter of the sugar and beat until stiff but not dry, set aside.

3 Combine cream, vanilla, and remaining sugar in another medium-size bowl and beat with mixer at high speed until stiff peaks form.

4 With rubber spatula, gently fold beaten egg white into whipped cream. Sprinkle mixture with 60 g (2 oz) of the gingersnap crumbs and fold in gently. Do *not* beat or overfold.

5 Divide mixture among four 250 g (8 oz) ramekins and tap each on counter to settle mixture. Cover each serving with waxed paper and freeze 1 1/2 to 2 hours, or until solid, or leave in freezer overnight.

6 Preheat oven to 180°C (350°F or Mark 4).

7 Arrange almonds in single layer on baking sheet and toast in oven, shaking pan occasionally to prevent scorching, 5 to 8 minutes, or until light golden.

8 Remove almonds from oven and set aside to cool slightly.

9 Just before serving, remove desserts from freezer and sprinkle each with toasted almonds. If desired, place in refrigerator for 10 minutes to soften.

Ann Burckhardt

Menu 1
(*Right*)
Vegetable Soup with Ham
Popovers
Creamy Cheddar Spread

Like most working mothers, Ann Burckhardt finds time a precious commodity. An early cooking mentor taught her to question the role each ingredient plays in a recipe: If an ingredient is not absolutely necessary, omit it and save the cost and the time needed to obtain, measure, and add it. For instance, the dough that wraps the hot dogs in Menu 2 consists of just two ingredients – self-raising flour and cream – rather than butter, flour, baking powder, salt, and water that a standard pastry might require.

All of Ann Burckhardt's menus reflect this efficient approach to cooking. Menu 1 is a simple meal that can be served at any time of year. The main-course soup – made with carrot, onion, courgette, and ham – is rich, yet light enough to be enjoyed in warm weather or cold. Here it is paired with airy popovers and a creamy Cheddar cheese spread.

In Menu 2, she offers hot dogs baked in pastry – more popularly known as pigs in blankets. When served with ketchup or chili sauce and mustard for dipping, they make ideal fare for a weekday supper or a child's birthday party. Corn on the cob cut into wheels and coleslaw with yogurt mayonnaise dressing are the perfect partners for the hot dogs.

Menu 3 has Swedish origins. Baked acorn squash halves are filled with tiny meatballs in a rich sauce and accompanied by scones flavoured with orange rind, anise, and fennel. The scones are an adaptation of the popular Scandinavian rye bread called *limpa*.

This family meal features an appetizing vegetable-ham soup and popovers with a mustardy Cheddar cheese spread. The popovers should be served hot, so seat everyone first, and then bring out the dinner.

Menu 1

Vegetable Soup with Ham
Popovers
Creamy Cheddar Spread

Popovers, unlike other quick breads, require no leavening agent to make them rise. They achieve their puffiness from the high proportion of liquid in the batter, which is converted to steam as the popovers bake in the hot oven. To get the most expansion, beat the batter until it has the consistency of heavy cream, and use a popover pan or aluminium muffin pan that has cups that are deeper than they are wide so the batter can expand only upward. Because popovers double in size when baked, very little batter is needed in each cup (divide the batter evenly among the cups, whether you use an 8-cup or a 12-cup pan). Preheating the pan sets the bottoms of the popovers and speeds the rising. Because popovers are fragile and can collapse if exposed to a sudden draft, do not open the oven door to peek at them until they are finished baking.

Start-to-Finish Steps

One hour ahead: Set out eggs for popovers recipe and butter and cheeses for Cheddar spread recipe to come to room temperature.

1 Follow Cheddar spread recipe steps 1 to 5.
2 Follow soup recipe steps 1 to 5.
3 Follow popovers recipe steps 1 to 7.
4 While popovers are baking, follow soup recipe steps 6 to 15.
5 Follow popovers recipe step 8, soup recipe step 16, and serve with Cheddar spread.

Vegetable Soup with Ham

2 large carrots (about 250 g (¹/₂ lb) total weight)
Medium-size courgette (about 250 g (¹/₂ lb))
Medium-size yellow onion
Small bunch parsley
625 ml (1¹/₄ pts) chicken stock
125 g (¹/₄ lb) cooked ham, sliced
6 level tablespoons unsalted butter
6 level tablespoons plain or unbleached flour
350 ml (12 fl oz) cups half-and-half milk and cream

1 Peel and trim carrots. Halve carrots lengthwise, then cut crosswise into 2¹/₂ cm (1 inch) pieces.
2 Scrub courgettes under cold running water and dry with paper towels. Trim ends and discard. Halve lengthwise, then cut crosswise into 2¹/₂ cm (1 inch) pieces.
3 Peel and quarter onion.
4 Using food processor or chef's knife, coarsely chop vegetables.
5 Wash parsley and dry with paper towels. Trim stems and discard. Mince enough parsley to measure 15 g (¹/₂ oz) and set aside; reserve remainder for another use.
6 Combine chopped vegetables and stock in medium-size saucepan and bring to a boil over medium-high heat. Reduce heat to medium, cover pan, and simmer about 10 minutes, or until vegetables are tender.
7 Meanwhile, stack ham slices and cut into thin strips.
8 Melt butter in stockpot over medium-high heat. Add ham strips and sauté, stirring frequently, 2 to 3 minutes.
9 With slotted spoon, transfer ham to small bowl and set aside.
10 Reduce heat under stockpot to low, add flour to butter remaining in pot, and whisk until blended. Cook mixture, stirring constantly, 30 seconds, or until it is smooth and bubbly.
11 Remove stockpot from heat. Whisking continuously, gradually add half-and-half and whisk until well blended and smooth.
12 Return stockpot to medium-high heat and bring soup base to a boil, stirring constantly. Boil 1 minute and remove pan from heat.

18

13 When vegetables are tender, pour stock through strainer set over medium-size bowl; set stock aside.

14 Turn cooked vegetables into container of food processor fitted with steel blade and pulse machine on and off once or twice to mince vegetables. Or, mince vegetables with chef's knife.

15 Stir minced vegetables, ham, and 500 ml (1 pt) of reserved stock into soup base and bring to a simmer over low heat.

16 Divide soup among 4 bowls, sprinkle each serving with parsley, and serve.

Popovers

300 ml (10 fl oz) milk
3 tablespoons vegetable oil, approximately
1/2 teaspoon salt
125 g (4 oz) plain or unbleached flour
30 g (1 oz) yellow cornmeal
3 large eggs, at room temperature

1 Preheat oven to 220°C (425°F or Mark 7).
2 Heat 8-cup heavy-gauge popover pan or 12-cup muffin pan in oven while preparing batter.
3 For batter, combine milk, 2 tablespoons oil, and salt in medium-size bowl.
4 Combine flour and cornmeal in sifter and sift into bowl with liquid ingredients. With wire whisk, beat mixture about 1 minute, or until smooth.
5 Add eggs, one at a time, beating after each addition just until incorporated; do *not* overbeat. Set batter aside.
6 Remove pan from oven and, using pastry brush, coat cups with remaining oil.
7 Divide batter among cups of popover or muffin pan and bake 20 to 25 minutes, or until popovers are puffed, golden, and crisp. Do not open oven door until popovers are ready.
8 Remove popovers from pan and serve. Do not cover them or they will become soggy.

Creamy Cheddar Spread

125 g (1/4 lb) sharp Cheddar cheese, at room temperature
Small yellow onion
250 g (8 oz) package cream cheese, at room temperature
2 level tablespoons unsalted butter, at room temperature
1 teaspoon Dijon mustard
1 1/2 teaspoons sweet Hungarian paprika, approximately

1 In food processor fitted with shredding disc, or with grater, shred Cheddar cheese. Transfer cheese to sheet of waxed paper.
2 Halve and peel onion. In food processor fitted with steel blade, or with chef's knife, mince enough onion to measure 1 tablespoon; reserve remaining onion for another use.
3 In food processor fitted with steel blade or in blender, combine shredded Cheddar, cream cheese, onion, milk, butter, and mustard, and process until smooth.
4 With machine running, add paprika, 1/4 teaspoon at a time, adding just enough to give mixture a rosy hue.
5 Divide cheese spread among 4 small ramekins or turn into small serving bowl, cover with plastic wrap, and refrigerate until ready to serve.

Leftover suggestion
Scoop any remaining cheese spread into an airtight container and refrigerate it for up to a week. The spread makes a zesty alternative to mayonnaise for sandwiches.

Pigs in Blankets
Corn Wheels
Coleslaw with Yogurt Mayonnaise

Youngsters and adults alike will love this all-American meal of pigs in blankets, corn wheels, and creamy coleslaw.

Corn on the cob is a food beloved by Americans of all ages. If possible, buy corn the same day it is picked, and cook it as soon as you can before its sugar turns to starch. No matter where you buy fresh corn, look for bright green husks and unwilted silk. The kernels should be of uniform colour and in regular rows, and the ears should have no odour. Cooking the corn in milk and butter keeps it sweet and tender.

Start-to-Finish Steps

1 Follow coleslaw recipe steps 1 to 5.
2 Follow pigs in blankets recipe step 1 and corn recipe step 1.
3 Follow pigs in blankets recipe steps 2 to 6.
4 While pigs in blankets are baking, follow corn recipe step 2 and coleslaw recipe step 6.
5 Follow corn recipe steps 3 and 4.
6 While butter is melting, follow pigs in blankets recipe step 7.
7 Follow coleslaw recipe step 7, pigs in blankets recipe step 8, corn recipe step 5, and serve.

Pigs in Blankets

125 g (4 oz) self-raising flour
175 ml (6 fl oz) heavy cream
8 hot dogs
400 g (14 oz) bottle ketchup or 350 g (12 oz) bottle chili sauce (optional)
250 g (8 oz) jar mustard (optional)

1 Preheat oven to 220°C (425°F or Mark 7).
2 In medium-size bowl, combine flour with enough cream to form a soft dough.
3 Turn dough out into lightly floured surface and knead twelve times.
4 Roll dough out into 18 by 25 cm (7 by 10 inch)

rectangle. Cut in half horizontally, then cut vertically into quarters, forming 8 'blankets.'

5 Place a hot dog along one short edge of a blanket, roll up, and seal tightly by pinching dough together. Place seam-side-down on ungreased baking pan. Repeat for remaining hot dogs.

6 Bake pigs in blankets 12 to 15 minutes, or until dough is golden brown.

7 Turn ketchup or chili sauce and mustard, if using, into individual serving bowls; set aside.

8 Transfer pigs in blankets to platter and serve with ketchup or chili sauce and mustard, if desired.

Corn Wheels

4 to 6 ears fresh corn on the cob
750 ml (1½ pts) low-fat milk
125 g (4 oz) unsalted butter

1 Shuck corn; remove and discard silk. Cut each ear crosswise into 3½ cm (1½ inch) wide 'wheels.'

2 Combine milk, 4 level tablespoons butter, and 1¼ ltrs (2 pts) water in large non-aluminium saucepan and bring to a boil over high heat.

3 Add corn and boil, partially covered, 5 to 8 minutes, or until fork tender.

4 Meanwhile, melt remaining butter in small heavy-gauge saucepan or butter warmer over low heat.

5 Using metal tongs, transfer corn to serving bowl and brush generously with melted butter.

Coleslaw with Yogurt Mayonnaise

Small head green cabbage (about 500 g (1 lb))
Large carrot
Small bunch scallions
60 ml (2 fl oz) plain yogurt
60 g (2 oz) mayonnaise
¼ teaspoon salt
30 g (1 oz) salted peanuts

1 Remove and discard bruised and discoloured outer leaves from cabbage. Quarter cabbage lengthwise; remove and discard core. Using food processor fitted with shredding disc, or coarse side of grater, shred enough cabbage to measure 300 g (10 oz); transfer to salad bowl. Reserve remaining cabbage for another use.

2 Peel and trim carrot. Using food processor fitted with steel blade, or coarse side of grater, shred enough carrot to measure 125 g (4 oz); add to bowl with cabbage.

3 Wash scallions and dry with paper towels. Trim ends and discard. Chop enough scallions to measure 2 level tablespoons; add to bowl with cabbage and shred carrot. Reserve remaining scallions for another use.

4 For dressing, combine yogurt, mayonnaise, and salt in small bowl and stir until well blended.

5 Add dressing to vegetables and toss until evenly coated. Cover with plastic wrap and refrigerate until ready to serve.

6 Coarsely chop peanuts; set aside.

7 Just before serving, sprinkle coleslaw with peanuts.

Menu 3

Swedish Meatballs in Acorn Squash
Limpa Scones

Apple-patterned dinnerware sets an autumn mood for acorn squash halves heaped with meatballs and gravy. Serve the honey-sweetened rye scones right from the oven in a napkin-lined basket.

Baking acorn squash preserves its full flavour. Select squash that is firm, heavy, and free of cracks or decay. You can fill the squash halves with the Swedish meatballs and sauce, or serve the filling separately.

Start-to-Finish Steps

1   Follow meatballs recipe steps 1 to 13 and increase oven temperature to 220°C (425°F or Mark 7).
2   Follow scones recipe steps 1 to 8.
3   Follow meatballs recipe step 14, scones recipe step 9, and serve.

Swedish Meatballs in Acorn Squash

2 small acorn squash (about 1 Kg (2 lb) total weight)
Small white or yellow onion
1 slice firm home-style bread
500 g (1 lb) minced beef
1 egg
250 ml (8 fl oz) milk
$^1/_2$ teaspoon freshly grated nutmeg
1 teaspoon salt
Freshly ground pepper
2 level tablespoons plus 2 teaspoons unsalted butter
3 level tablespoons plain flour
250 ml (8 fl oz) beef stock
125 ml (4 fl oz) heavy cream

1   Preheat oven to 200°C (400°F or Mark 6).
2   Halve squash lengthwise; scoop out seeds and strings, and discard. Place squash halves cut-side-down in 28 by 18 by 3$^1/_2$ cm (11 by 7 by 1$^1/_2$ inch) baking pan. Fill pan to a depth of 5 mm ($^1/_4$ inch) with hot tap water and bake squash, uncovered, 30 minutes, or until fork tender.
3   Meanwhile, peel and quarter onion. In food processor fitted with steel blade, chop enough onion to measure 60 g (2 oz). Or, mince onion with chef's knife and place in large bowl.
4   Trim crusts from bread and discard. Tear bread into small pieces and add to onions.
5   Crumble meat and add to onions and bread.
6   Add egg, milk, and nutmeg to meat mixture in processor, season with salt and pepper, and pulse

22

machine on and off a few times, just until mixture is combined. Or, blend mixture with your hands; do *not* overwork mixture.

7   Heat 2 tablespoons butter in large heavy-gauge skillet or 1 tablespoon butter in each of 2 medium-size skillets over medium-high heat.

8   While butter is heating, begin shaping meatballs: Using two teaspoons, scoop up a heaped teaspoonful of meat mixture in one spoon, then roll meat off spoon into skillet with second teaspoon. Working quickly, repeat process with remaining meat mixture. You will have approximately 28 meatballs. Brown meatballs, turning occasionally with small spatula, about 15 minutes, or until evenly browned.

9   With slotted spoon, transfer meatballs to ovenproof casserole and pour fat from skillet into small heatproof bowl.

10 Return 2 tablespoons fat to skillet. Whisk in flour and cook mixture over medium heat, whisking constantly, 1 to 2 minutes, or until bubbly.

11 Add stock to skillet and continue cooking, stirring occasionally, about 3 minutes, or until sauce thickens.

12 Reduce heat to low, add cream. and whisk until blended. Pour sauce over meatballs, cover casserole, and keep warm on stove top until ready to serve.

13 When squash is done, remove from oven and turn cut side-up. Using paring knife, crosshatch flesh of each half and dot each with ¹/₂ teaspoon butter. Cover loosely with aluminium foil and keep warm on stove top until ready to serve.

14 Divide squash halves among 4 dinner plates and fill cavity of each with meatballs and sauce.

Limpa Scones

60 ml (2 fl oz) plus 1 tablespoon vegetable oil
1 orange
1 teaspoon fennel seeds
¹/₂ teaspoon anise seeds
125 g (4 oz) self-raising flour
125 g (4 oz) medium rye flour
¹/₄ teaspoon baking soda
1 egg
2 tablespoons honey or molasses
175 ml (6 fl oz) buttermilk

1   Lightly grease a large baking sheet; set aside.

2   Wash orange and dry with paper towel. Grate enough orange rind to measure 1 level tablespoon; set aside. Reserve orange for another use.

3   Crush fennel and anise seeds in mortar with pestle. Or, place seeds between 2 sheets of waxed paper and crush with rolling pin. Set seeds aside.

4   Sift self-raising and rye flours into medium-size bowl. Stir in baking soda; set aside.

5   In small bowl, beat egg with fork just until blended. Stir in 60 ml (2 fl oz) vegetable oil, honey or molasses, buttermilk, crushed fennel seeds, anise seeds, and grated orange rind.

6   Add buttermilk mixture to dry ingredients and mix quickly with fork, until mixture holds together.

7   Using sharp knife, cut dough in half. Turn half the dough out onto one corner of prepared baking sheet; turn other half out onto opposite corner of sheet. With floured fingers, pat dough out into two 20 cm (8 inch) rounds, about 1 cm (¹/₂ inch) thick. With knife dipped in flour, cut each round into 6 wedges, but do not separate.

8   Bake scones in preheated 220°C (425°F or Mark 7) oven 10 to 15 minutes, or until lightly browned.

9   Remove scones from oven, separate wedges, and turn into napkin-lined basket.

23

Lucy Wing

Menu 1
(*Right*)
Tex-Mex Macaroni and Cheese
California Salad
Mexican Hot Chocolate

Although Lucy Wing grew up eating traditional Chinese food, she describes herself as an eclectic cook with an international palate. She particularly enjoys simplifying recipes from many lands and cooking quickly to preserve the natural flavours of foods. Her family menus feature basic dishes with some new twists.

In Menu 1, macaroni and cheese, an all-American favourite, takes on south-western flair with the addition of diced mild green chilis and a topping of tomato sauce, grated cheese, scallions, and olives. An avocado and vegetable salad and Mexican-style hot chocolate are served with the casserole.

Menu 2 and 3 will please children and adults alike. Menu 2 offers grilled steak marinated in a tangy vinegar and herb mixture. The cook accompanies the meat with her own version of home fries in which the potato slices are sautéed and then baked for extra crispness.

Menu 3 is a quick easy midweek meal that features whole-wheat pizza made with a quick-bread crust that does not require time to rise. The pizza is topped with a variety of traditional ingredients – mozzarella cheese, tomato sauce, mushrooms, green peppers, and pepperoni – and presented with a colourful three-bean salad.

Bright tableware sets off this colourful south-western meal of macaroni and cheese casserole and California-style salad. Mugs of spiced Mexican hot chocolate add sweetness.

Menu 1

Tex-Mex Macaroni and Cheese
California Salad
Mexican Hot Chocolate

For the macaroni and cheese dish, the cook prefers mild Cheddar.

The fitting beverage for this Tex-Mex meal is Mexican-style hot chocolate, which is spiced with cinnamon and whisked before serving. For an extra-frothy drink, pour one cup of the hot chocolate into a blender and whip until foamy. Return the beaten chocolate to the pan, add the vanilla, and serve.

Start-to-Finish Steps
1 Follow hot chocolate recipe step 1.
2 Follow salad recipe steps 1 to 7.
3 follow hot chocolate recipe step 2.
4 Follow macaroni recipe steps 1 to 17.
5 Follow hot chocolate recipe steps 3 to 5.
6 Follow salad recipe step 8, macaroni recipe step 18, and serve with hot chocolate.

Tex-Mex Macaroni and Cheese

250 g (½ lb) mild Cheddar cheese
125 g (4 oz) can diced mild green chilis
250 g (8 oz) macaroni
2 level tablespoons unsalted butter
3 level tablespoons plain flour
1 teaspoon dry mustard
½ teaspoon salt
500 ml (1 pt) milk
1 teaspoon Worcestershire sauce
Small bunch scallions
1 tablespoon olive or vegetable oil
1 teaspoon chili powder
250 g (8 oz) can tomato sauce
100 g (3 oz) pitted black olives (optional)

1 Preheat oven to 190°C (375°F or Mark 5).
2 Bring 3½ ltrs (6 pts) water to a boil in large saucepan or stockpot over high heat.
3 While water is heating, shred enough cheese in food processor fitted with shredding disc, or with grater, to measure 250 g (8 oz); set aside.
4 Turn chilis into strainer and rinse under cold running water. Drain and pat dry with paper towels. Set aside 3 to 4 tablespoons chilis and reserve remainder for another use.
5 Add macaroni to boiling water, stir to separate, and cook 8 to 12 minutes, or according to package directions.
6 Meanwhile, melt butter in medium-size non-aluminium saucepan over medium heat. Whisk in flour, mustard, and salt.
7 Remove pan from heat. Whisking continuously, gradually add milk and whisk until well blended.
8 Return pan to heat and cook, stirring constantly, 2 to 3 minutes, or until sauce thickens.
9 Reduce heat to low and simmer sauce 1 minute.
10 Meanwhile, grease shallow 2 ltr (3½ pt) baking dish; set aside.
11 Remove sauce from heat. Stir in 175 g (6 oz) shredded cheese, chilis, and Worcestershire sauce, and continue stirring 1 to 2 minutes, or until cheese is completely melted; set aside.
12 Turn macaroni into colander and drain. Return macaroni to large saucepan or stockpot, add cheese sauce, and toss to combine.
13 Turn macaroni and cheese into prepared baking

dish, smooth top, and bake 25 to 30 minutes, or until sauce is bubbly.

14 Meanwhile, wash scallions and dry with paper towels. Trim ends and discard. finely chop enough scallions to measure 30 g (1 oz), and cut enough remaining scallions crosswise into 5 mm ($^1/_4$ inch) pieces to measure 30 g (1 oz) for garnish, if using. Reserve any remaining scallions for another use.

15 Heat oil in small non-aluminium saucepan over medium heat. Add 30 g (1 oz) chopped scallions and chili powder, and sauté 1 minute.

16 Stir in tomato sauce and bring to a boil. Reduce heat to low and simmer, partially covered, 10 minutes.

17 Drain olives, if using, and slice; set aside.

18 Remove baked macaroni from oven, spoon tomato sauce over centre, and top with remaining cheese. Sprinkle with scallion pieces and olive slices if desired, and serve.

California Salad

Large lemon
100 ml (3 fl oz) olive oil or vegetable oil
$^1/_2$ teaspoon dried tarragon
$^1/_4$ teaspoon salt
Dash of Cayenne pepper
1 head iceberg lettuce
Large ripe avocado, preferably Hass variety
Small cucumber
Small bunch red radishes

1 Halve lemon crosswise and squeeze enough juice to measure 3 tablespoons.

2 To prepare dressing, combine 2 tablespoons lemon juice, oil, tarragon, salt, and Cayenne pepper in small jar with tight-fitting lid, and shake until well blended; set aside.

3 Remove any bruised or discoloured outer leaves from lettuce. Halve lettuce lengthwise; cut out core from each half and discard. Rinse lettuce under cold running water and dry in salad spinner or with paper towels. Cut enough lettuce crosswise into 5 mm ($^1/_4$ inch) wide shreds to measure about 500 g (1 lb). Divide lettuce among 4 salad plates; set aside.

4 Halve avocado lengthwise. Twist halves to separate; remove and discard pit. Peel avocado. Cut each half lengthwise into 8 slices and arrange in single layer on large plate. Sprinkle avocado with remaining lemon juice to prevent discolouration and turn slices to coat evenly. Divide avocado slices among lettuce-lined plates.

5 Wash cucumber and dry with paper towel. With fork, score peel lengthwise. Cut enough cucumber crosswise into 5 mm ($^1/_4$ inch) thick slices to measure 100 g (3 oz). Top each salad with equal portions of cucumber slices.

6 Wash and trim radishes; dry with paper towels. Cut enough radishes crosswise into 5 mm ($^1/_4$ inch) thick slices to measure 60 g (2 oz) and divide among salads. Reserve remaining radishes for another use.

7 Cover salads with plastic wrap and refrigerate until ready to serve.

8 Just before serving, shake dressing to recombine and pour an equal amount over each salad.

Mexican Hot Chocolate

125 ml (4 fl oz) heavy cream
60 g (2 oz) (2 squares) semisweet chocolate
$^1/_2$ teaspoon cinnamon
60 g (2 oz) sugar, approximately
1$^1/_4$ ltrs (2 pts) milk
1 teaspoon vanilla extract

1 Place small bowl and beaters for whipping cream in freezer to chill, about 10 minutes.

2 Pour cream into chilled bowl and beat with electric mixer at high speed until stiff. Cover with plastic wrap and refrigerate until ready to serve.

3 Melt chocolate in medium-size heavy-gauge saucepan over low heat.

4 Whisk in cinnamon, and sugar to taste. Whisking continuously, add milk gradually and heat about 5 minutes, or until chocolate is hot and slightly foamy.

5 Stir in vanilla extract. Divide hot chocolate among 4 mugs and top each serving with a dollop of whipped cream.

Herb-Marinated Steak
Home Fries
Grilled Summer Squash and Tomatoes

Steak and potatoes are always a good family meal. Here the potatoes are left unpeeled to save time and to preserve the nutrients found just beneath the potato skins. After sautéing, the potatoes finish browning in the oven and need no further attention.

Courgette and yellow squash are at their peak during the summer, but are often available in supermarkets in other seasons. You can use courgette alone, if necessary. Select small, plump squash with

glossy, unblemished skins. Avoid any that are very large; they tend to be bland and seedy. If you must purchase the squash a few days in advance, store them in a perforated plastic bag in the refrigerator.

Start-to-Finish Steps

1 Follow steak recipe step 1 and home fries recipe steps 1 to 5.
2 While potatoes are baking, follow vegetables recipe steps 1 to 4.
3 Follow home fries recipe step 6 and vegetables recipe steps 5 to 10.
4 Follow steak recipe steps 2 to 5 and serve with home fries and vegetables.

Turn a family dinner into a special occasion with marinated grilled steak – cooked indoors or out – accompanied by golden-brown potato slices and bread-crumb-topped summer vegetables. Tumblers of iced tea refresh the palate.

Herb-Marinated Steak

100 ml (3 fl oz) red wine vinegar
100 ml (3 fl oz) soy sauce
100 ml (3 fl oz) Worcestershire sauce
60 g (2 oz) light brown sugar
1 teaspoon dried oregano
$^1/_2$ teaspoon dried basil
750 g (1$^1/_2$ lbs) 1 cm (1 inch) thick boneless sirloin
    steak

1   Combine vinegar, soy sauce, Worcestershire sauce,
    brown sugar, oregano, and basil in 33 by 23 by 5
    cm (13 by 9 by 2 inch) glass or ceramic dish. Add
    steak and set aside to marinate about 30 minutes
    at room temperature.
2   Transfer steak to grill rack set 10 cm (4 inches)
    from heating element in preheated grill and grill
    on one side, 7 minutes for rare, 8 minutes for
    medium, or 10 minutes for well done. Reserve
    marinade.

3   Using metal tongs, turn steak, brush with marinade,
    and grill another 7 to 10 minutes for desired degree
    of doneness.
4   Transfer steak to serving platter, cover loosely
    with foil, and allow to rest 5 minutes.
5   Slice steak and serve.

Home Fries

1 kg (2 lbs) waxy potatoes
4 level tablespoons unsalted butter
4 tablespoons olive oil
Salt and freshly ground black pepper

1   Preheat oven to 240°F (475°F or Mark 9).
2   With vegetable brush, scrub potatoes under cold
    running water. Rinse and dry with paper towels;
    do *not* peel. Cut potatoes crosswise into 2$^1/_2$ mm
    ($^1/_8$ inch) thick slices; set aside.
3   Heat butter and oil in large sauté pan over medium

heat. Add half the potato slices and fry, turning with spatula, 2 to 3 minutes, or just until slices are evenly coated with fat and beginning to soften.

4 With slotted spatula, transfer fried potatoes to small shallow baking dish; reserve fat in pan. Season fried potatoes with salt and pepper and repeat with remaining potatoes, placing second batch on top of first when fried.

5 Bake potatoes, uncovered, about 20 minutes, or until fork-tender.

6 Remove potatoes from oven, cover loosely with foil, and keep warm on stove top until ready to serve.

Grilled Summer Squash and Tomatoes

2 small courgettes (about 350 g (³/₄ lb) total weight)
2 small yellow squash (about 350 g (³/₄ lb) total weight)
4 small tomatoes (about 350 g (³/₄ lb) total weight)
Small clove garlic
5 level tablespoons unsalted butter
30 g (1 oz) seasoned dry bread crumbs
Salt and freshly ground black pepper

1 Scrub courgette and yellow squash under cold running water; rinse and dry with paper towels. Trim ends and discard. Halve each squash lengthwise; set aside.

2 Wash tomatoes and dry with paper towels. Cut 1 cm (¹/₂ inch) thick slice from top of each tomato and, using sharp paring knife, cut around top in zigzag pattern; set tomatoes aside.

3 Peel and mince garlic; set aside.

4 Melt butter in small saucepan over low heat; set aside.

5 Preheat grill.

6 Brush cut sides of squash halves with some of the butter, place cut-side-down on grill rack set 3 inches from heating element, and grill 5 minutes.

7 Turn squash and grill another 3 minutes.

8 Meanwhile, stir garlic, bread crumbs, and salt and pepper to taste into remaining butter.

9 Add tomatoes to grill rack with squash, sprinkle all vegetables with crumb mixture, and grill another 2 minutes, or just until crumbs are golden brown.

10 Carefully transfer vegetables to platter. Cover loosely with foil and keep warm on stove top until ready to serve.

Added touch
Profiteroles, or cream puffs, need not be intimidating to make. The pastry shells are foolproof if you do not overheat or overbeat the flour-butter mixture during its initial cooking; if cooked too long, the water that creates the steam for puffing evaporates.

Profiteroles

30 g (1 oz) sliced almonds (optional)
4 level tablespoons unsalted butter
60 g (2 oz) unsifted plain flour
2 large eggs, at room temperature
125 ml (4 fl oz) heavy cream
60 g (2 oz) semisweet chocolate chips
500 ml (1 pt) vanilla ice cream

1 Preheat oven to 180°C (350°F or Mark 4).

2 If using almonds, spread on baking sheet and toast in oven, shaking pan occasionally to prevent scorching, 5 to 8 minutes, or until light golden.

3 Meanwhile, heat butter and 125 ml (4 fl oz) water in small saucepan over medium heat until butter melts. Add flour all at once and stir vigorously with wooden spoon about 1 minute, or until mixture is well blended and forms a smooth ball. Remove from heat.

4 Remove almonds from oven and set aside to cool. Increase oven temperature to 200°C (400°F or Mark 6).

5 Add eggs to flour mixture, 1 at a time, beating after each addition until mixture is smooth.

6 Drop dough in 8 mounds, about 5 cm (2 inches) apart, onto ungreased cookie sheet and bake 20 to 25 minutes, or until puffed and golden brown.

7 Meanwhile, combine cream and chocolate chips in small heavy-gauge saucepan and bring to a boil over medium-low heat, stirring continuously with wooden spoon.

8 Reduce heat to low and cook another 2 to 3 minutes, stirring, or until mixture is slightly thickened.

9 Remove pan from heat and set mixture aside to cool to room temperature.

10 When done, transfer baked puffs to wire rack to cool.

11 Just before serving, cut tops off puffs and remove any uncooked dough from centres. Fill puffs with ice cream, replace tops, and place on platter, or divide among 4 dessert plates. Top each puff with chocolate sauce and sprinkle with toasted almond slices, if desired. Serve any remaining sauce separately.

'The Works' Whole-Wheat Pizza
Mixed Bean Salad

This no-yeast pizza crust has a quick-bread texture. After combining the dough ingredients, you roll out the dough right in the pizza pan; no tedious kneading or stretching is necessary. Use any or all of the toppings suggested here, or select others that your family might like better.

Start-to-Finish Steps

1 Follow salad recipe steps 1 to 7.
2 Follow pizza recipe steps 1 to 14 and serve with salad.

Whole-wheat pizza with a variety of toppings and a mixed bean salad make a quick, light supper just right for family or friends.

'The Works' Whole-Wheat Pizza

2 level tablespoons cornmeal
150-175 g (5-6 oz) unsifted plain flour
60 g (2 oz) whole-wheat flour
1 tablespoon baking powder
$\frac{1}{2}$ teaspoon salt
150-175 ml (5-6 fl oz) milk
60 ml (2 fl oz) plus 2 tablespoons vegetable oil
Large egg
250 g (8 oz) package mozzarella cheese
125 g (4 oz) medium-size mushrooms
250 ml (8 fl oz) spaghetti sauce
Small green bell pepper
16 slices pepperoni

1 Preheat oven to 230°C (450°F or Mark 8).
2 Grease 33 or 38 cm (13 or 15 inch) pizza pan and sprinkle bottom with cornmeal. Tilt and rotate pan until evenly coated; discard excess.
3 In large bowl, combine plain flour, whole-wheat flour, baking powder, and salt, and stir with fork to blend; set aside.
4 Combine milk, oil, and egg in small bowl and stir with fork until well blended.
5 Stirring with wooden spoon, gradually add milk mixture to dry ingredients and stir until a soft, moist dough forms. If dough is too sticky to gather into a ball, gradually add more flour; if too dry, add more milk.
6 Turn dough onto prepared pan and flatten to $2\frac{1}{2}$ cm (1 inch) thickness. Remove waxed paper and, with floured fingertips, pinch dough around edge

to form 1 cm ($\frac{1}{2}$ inch) raised rim. Bake pizza crust 15 minutes, or until lightly browned.
7 Meanwhile, in food processor fitted with shredding disc, or with grater, shred cheese; set aside.
8 Wipe mushrooms clean with damp paper towels. Trim stems and discard. Cut mushrooms into $2\frac{1}{2}$ mm ($\frac{1}{8}$ inch) thick slices; set aside. Line plate with double thickness of paper towels.
9 Heat remaining 2 tablespoons oil in medium-size skillet over medium-high heat. Add mushrooms and sauté, stirring, 1 minute, or just until wilted.
10 With slotted spoon, transfer mushrooms to paper-towel lined plate to drain; set aside.
11 Remove crust from oven and sprinkle with half the cheese. Spoon spaghetti sauce over cheese and, with back of spoon, spread evenly over crust. Top with remaining cheese and sprinkle with mushrooms. Bake pizza another 10 to 15 minutes, or until crust is browned and cheese is bubbly.
12 Meanwhile, wash, core and seed green pepper. Cut lengthwise into at least 16 strips; set aside.
13 Remove pizza from oven. Top with pepper strips and pepperoni, and return to oven for a few minutes to warm pepperoni and peppers.
14 Remove pizza from oven and cut into 8 wedges. Divide among 4 dinner plates and serve.

Mixed Bean Salad

250 g ($\frac{1}{2}$ lb) green beans, or 500g (1 lb) if not using yellow (wax) beans
250 g ($\frac{1}{2}$ lb) yellow (Wax) beans, if available
Small red onion
500g (1 lb) can red kidney beans
60 ml (2 fl oz) olive oil
3 tablespoons red wine vinegar
$\frac{3}{4}$ teaspoon salt
Pinch of freshly ground pepper
1 to $1\frac{1}{2}$ level tablespoons sugar

1 Bring $2\frac{1}{2}$ ltrs (4 pts) water to a boil in large saucepan.
2 Meanwhile, trim stem ends of fresh beans. Cut beans crosswise into $2\frac{1}{2}$ cm (1 inch) pieces and add to boiling water. After water returns to a boil, cook beans, uncovered, 1 to 2 minutes, or until crisp-tender.
3 Transfer beans to colander, refresh under cold running water, and set aside to drain.
4 Peel onion and cut crosswise into $2\frac{1}{2}$ mm ($\frac{1}{8}$ inch) thick slices.
5 Rinse kidney beans in large strainer; drain thoroughly.

6 Combine all the beans and the onion slices in large bowl and toss to combine; set aside.

7 For dressing, combine oil, vinegar, salt, pepper, and sugar to taste in small bowl, and beat with fork until blended. Pour dressing over beans and toss until evenly coated. Cover and refrigerate until ready to serve.

Added touches

For a smooth and thick custard sauce, use a heavy-gauge saucepan to assure even heat distribution.

Fresh Fruit Cup with Custard Sauce

500 g (1 lb) strawberries
125 g (4 oz) seedless green grapes
1 lemon
Small banana
Custard sauce (see following recipe)

1 Rinse, dry, and hull strawberries. Cut any very large berries into pieces.

2 Wash and dry grapes. Halve lengthwise; set aside.

3 Squeeze enough lemon juice to measure 1 tablespoon.

4 Peel banana in small bowl and sprinkle with lemon juice to prevent discolouration; toss gently until evenly coated.

5 Divide fruit among 4 small bowls or cups, top with custard sauce, and serve.

Custard Sauce

125 ml (4 fl oz) milk
2 egg yolks, at room temperature
2 level tablespoons sugar
2 tablespoons Marsala, or $1/2$ teaspoon vanilla extract

1 Heat milk in small heavy-gauge non-aluminium saucepan over low heat about 3 minutes, or just until small bubbles appear around edge of pan.

2 Meanwhile, combine egg yolks and sugar in small bowl and beat with electric hand mixer at high speed 1 to 2 minutes, or until light and fluffy.

3 Beating at low speed, gradually add scalded milk and beat until totaly incorporated.

4 Return mixture to saucepan and cook over low heat, beating continuously with hand mixer at low speed, 2 to 3 minutes, or until custard thickens slightly. Simmer sauce 1 minute.

5 Add Marsala or vanilla extract and beat at medium speed 5 minutes, or until mixture holds its shape slightly when dropped from a spoon; do *not* overcook.

6 Remove pan from heat and cover until ready to serve.

Amaretti, Italian almond macaroons, are the perfect accompaniment for fruit desserts.

Amaretti

200 g (7 oz) roll almond paste
2 egg whites
$1/4$ teaspoon almond extract
125 g (4 oz) granulated sugar
125 g (4 oz) can natural almond slices for garnish (optional)

1 Preheat oven to 150°C (300°F or Mark 2).

2 Line 2 cookie sheets with parchment paper or foil.

3 Crumble almond paste into small bowl. Add egg whites and almond extract, and beat with electric mixer at medium speed 3 minutes, or until well blended.

4 Still beating, add sugar slowly and beat until smooth.

5 Drop dough by rounded teaspoons, about 2 inches apart, onto cookie sheets. You will have about $2^{1}/2$ dozen cookies. Garnish each with an almond slice, if desired, and bake 20 minutes, or until firm and lightly browned.

6 Transfer paper or foil with amaretti to racks to cool.

7 Peel off paper, transfer amaretti to platter, and serve.

Jane Kirby

Menu 1
(*Left*)
Cheese and Prosciutto Calzoni
Green Beans and Onions Vinaigrette
Carrots with Orange-Honey Dressing

As a dietitian, Jane Kirby is committed to serving wholesome meals, but she is not an advocate of health foods, megavitamins, or nutritional fads. She believes that people are best nourished by eating a wide variety of foods and that there are no such things as 'kids' foods' and 'adults foods.' At her house, even French fries and banana splits are allowed because they are part of good square meals. All three of her menus are planned not only for nutritional balance but also for flavour and appearance.

Neapolitan *calzoni*, or pizza turnovers, filled with a blend of three mild cheeses and prosciutto, are the fun-to-eat main course of Menu 1. This easy-to-prepare meal also features green beans vinaigrette and carrots with a honey and orange dressing.

Menu 2 offers meaty loin pork chops, which the cook skillet-braises for about half an hour in orange juice spiced with cloves. The chops are accompanied by a bulgur pilaf flecked with orange peel, raisins, and almonds, and by peas flavoured with garlic and mint.

Menu 3 is another delicious meal that the whole family will ask for time and again. Boned and skinned chicken breasts are quickly sautéed, then topped with a subtle honey-lime sauce. With the chicken, Jane Kirby serves corn mixed with bell peppers and onion, and tasty butter-milk-Cheddar biscuits.

Golden calzoni *filled with cheese and prosciutto go well with two vegetable salads – carrots with orange zest, and green beans and onions vinaigrette. Iced tea garnished with lemon slices is refreshing with this meal.*

Menu 1

Cheese and Prosciutto Calzoni
Green Beans and Onions Vinaigrette
Carrots with Orange-Honey Dressing

Portable pizzas, *calzoni* are perfect for cook-outs as well as for casual indoor suppers: Just reheat them over the coals as you would in the oven. The *calzoni* filling is made with mozzarella, ricotta, and Parmesan cheese mixed with prosciutto, a dry-cured unsmoked ham with a dark pink colour and mild flavour. Prosciutto is available at most supermarkets and Italian groceries.

Start-to-Finish Steps

Four hours ahead: Set out frozen bread dough to thaw for calzoni recipe.

1 Follow beans and onions recipe steps 1 to 4.
2 Wash parsley and dry with paper towels. Trim ends and discard. Mince enough parsley to measure 2 tablespoons for calzoni recipe and 3 tablespoons for beans and onions recipe. Reserve remainder for another use.
3 Follow beans and onions recipe steps 5 and 6.
4 Follow carrots recipe steps 1 to 6.
5 Follow calzoni recipe steps 1 to 10, beans and onions recipe step 7, carrots recipe step 7, and serve.

Cheese and Prosciutto Calzoni

250 g (8 oz) can whole tomatoes
250 g (8 oz) package mozzarella cheese
60 g (2 oz) Parmesan cheese
60 g (2 oz) prosciutto or baked ham
Small red onion
250 g (8 oz) container ricotta cheese
2 level tablespoons minced fresh parsley
Freshly ground black pepper
2 level tablespoons plain flour, approximately
500 g (1 lb) loaf frozen bread dough, thawed
1 tablespoon olive or vegetable oil, approximately
1 teaspoon dried oregano

1 Turn tomatoes into strainer set over small bowl and drain well; reserve liquid for another use. Gently squeeze tomatoes to remove seeds. Chop tomatoes; set aside.
2 Halve mozzarella crosswise. Using food processor

fitted with shredding disc, or coarse side of grater, shred one half of mozzarella; reserve remaining half for another use.
3 Using grater, grate enough Parmesan cheese to measure 2 tablespoons; set aside.
4 With chef's knife, finely chop prosciutto or ham.
5 Halve and peel onion. Mince enough onion to measure 60 g (2 oz); set aside. Reserve remaining onion for another use.
6 For filling, combine tomatoes, mozzarella, Parmesan, ham, onion, ricotta, parsley, and pepper to taste in medium-size bowl and stir with fork to blend.
7 Preheat oven to 200°C (400°F or Mark 6).
8 On floured surface, roll out one-quarter of dough into 15 cm (6 inch) round, 5-10 mm ($^{1}/_{4}$-$^{1}/_{2}$ inch) thick) with lightly floured rolling pin. Spoon one-quarter of filling onto one side of the dough, leaving a 2$^{1}/_{2}$ cm (1 inch) border around edge. Moisten edge with water, fold dough over filling so that edges meet, and press to seal; transfer to ungreased baking sheet. Repeat with remaining dough and filling, making 4 calzoni in all.
9 Bake calzoni 15 to 18 minutes, or until golden.
10 Removed baked calzoni from oven, brush each with oil, and sprinkle with oregano. With metal spatula, transfer calzoni to 4 dinner plates and serve.

Green Beans and Onions Vinaigrette

500 g (1 lb) green beans
Medium-size yellow or white onion

Dressing:
125 ml (4 fl oz) olive or vegetable oil
100 ml (3 fl oz) cider vinegar
1 level tablespoon Dijon mustard
3 level tablespoons minced fresh parsley
$^{1}/_{4}$ teaspoon salt
Pinch of freshly ground black pepper

1 Trim ends from beans. Place beans in colander and rinse under cold running water; set aside.

2 Peel onion and cut crosswise into 5 mm (¹/₄ inch) thick slices. Separate into rings; set aside.
3 Fill bottom of steamer unit, or saucepan large enough to accommodate collapsible steamer, with enough cold water to come up to but not over steamer basket and bring to a boil over high heat.
4 Add beans and onions to steamer, cover pan, and steam about 6 minutes, or until vegetables are crisp-tender.
5 Turn vegetables into colander and refresh under cold running water. Drain well and dry with paper towels. Place vegetables in medium-size non-aluminium bowl.
6 Combine dressing ingredients in small jar with lid and shake until evenly coated; set aside until ready to serve.
7 Using slotted spoon, divide green beans and onions among dinner plates and serve.

Carrots with Orange-Honey Dressing

500 g (1 lb) baby carrots or medium-size carrots
Medium-size orange
100 ml (3 fl oz) olive or vegetable oil
2 tablespoons honey
¹/₂ teaspoon salt
Pinch of fresh ground black pepper

1 Peel and trim carrots. If using medium-size carrots, cut crosswise into thirds, then halve pieces lengthwise.
2 Fill steamer unit, or saucepan large enough to accommodate collapsible steamer, with enough cold water to come up to but not over steamer basket and bring to a boil over high heat.
3 Add carrots to steamer and cook about 8 minutes, or until crisp-tender.
4 Meanwhile, wash and dry orange. Using grater, grate enough rind to measure 1 level tablespoon, then squeeze enough juice to measure 125 ml (4 fl oz); set both aside.
5 Turn carrots into colander and refresh under cold running water. Drain and dry with paper towels. Place carrots in medium-size non-aluminium bowl.
6 In small jar with tight-fitting lid, combine grated orange rind, orange juice, and remaining ingredients, and shake until well blended. Pour over carrots and toss until evenly coated; set aside until ready to serve.
7 Using slotted spoon, divide carrots among dinner plates and serve.

Added touch
These delicate, spicy cookies will be a welcome addition to the family cookie jar.

Chocolate-Cinnamon Wafers

300 g (10 oz) plain flour
2 teaspoons baking powder
1¹/₂ teaspoons cinnamon
¹/₂ teaspoon salt
125 g (4 oz) unsalted butter or margarine, at room temperature
300 g (10 oz) granulated sugar
2 eggs, at room temperature
1 teaspoon vanilla extract
60 g (2 oz) unsweetened cocoa powder

1 Combine flour, baking powder, cinnamon, and salt in medium-size bowl, and stir with fork until well blended.
2 Combine butter and sugar in another medium-size bowl and beat with electric mixer at medium speed until fluffy.
3 One at a time, add eggs, beating after each addition until totaly incorporated.
4 Add vanilla and continue beating, occasionally scraping down sides of bowl with rubber spatula, until mixture is light and fluffy.
5 Stir in cocoa, then gradually add other dry ingredients, stirring until well blended.
6 Shape dough into ball, wrap in waxed paper, and refrigerate for several hours, or until firm and easy to handle
7 Preheat oven to 190°C (375°F or Mark 5).
8 Place about one-fifth of dough directly on ungreased cookie sheet and roll out very thinly. With a 5 cm (2¹/₂ inch) cookie cutter, cut out cookies, leaving about 2¹/₂ cm (1 inch) between them. Remove dough between cookies and bake cookies 8 to 10 minutes.
9 Transfer cookies to wire rack to cool completely.
10 Recombine dough scraps and repeat with remaining dough, rechilling dough, if necessary, for easier handling. You will have about 90 cookies.

<table>
<tr><td>

</td><td>

Pork Chops with Orange Sauce
Bulgur Pilaf
Peas with Mint

</td></tr>
</table>

The flavours of orange and mint predominate in this simple dinner of braised pork chops with orange sauce, bulgur with raisins, almonds, and orange zest, and peas with mint. For an appealing garnish, twist an orange slice into an S shape.

For this meal, bulgur pilaf is served as an accompaniment to the pork. Sometimes mistakenly called cracked wheat, bulgur is whole-wheat berries that are steam-cooked, dried, and then ground.

Start-to-Finish Steps
One hour ahead: Set out frozen peas to thaw.

1 Wash 1 juice orange and dry with paper towel. Using grater, grate enough rind, avoiding white pith as much as possible, to measure 1 tablespoon for pilaf recipe. Squeeze enough juice oranges to measure 175 ml (6 fl oz) for pork chops recipe.
2 Follow pork chops recipe steps 1 to 6.
3 Follow pilaf recipe steps 1 to 4.
4 Follow peas recipe steps 1 to 6.
5 Follow pork chops recipe steps 7 and 8.
6 Follow pilaf recipe steps 5 and 6.
7 Follow pork chops recipe steps 9 and 10 and serve with pilaf and peas.

Pork Chops with Orange Sauce

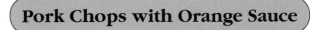

Four 2½ cm (1 inch) thick loin pork chops (about 850 g (1¾ lbs) total weight)
175 ml (6 fl oz) freshly squeezed orange juice
1 teaspoon sugar
1 teaspoon salt
1 teaspoon whole cloves
½ teaspoon cornstarch
Medium-size navel orange for garnish (optional)

1 Trim excess fat from pork chops; reserve fat.
2 Place large heavy-gauge skillet over medium-high heat and run pork fat over bottom to grease it; discard fat.
3 Add chops; cook 4 minutes per side, or until browned.
4 Add orange juice, sugar, salt, and cloves to skillet, increase heat to high, and bring to a boil. Reduce heat to low, cover, and simmer 25 to 30 minutes, or until chops are fork-tender.
5 Meanwhile, combine cornstarch and 2 tablespoons water in measuring cup and stir until cornstarch dissolves.
6 Wash and dry navel orange, if using. Cut four 5 mm (¼ inch) thick slices crosswise from orange.

7 Transfer chops to heatproof platter and keep warm in 200°C (400°F or Mark 6) oven.

8 Spoon off fat from skillet. Boil remaining liquid over high heat about 10 minutes, or until reduced by half.

9 Add cornstarch mixture to liquid in skillet and whisk until blended. Continue to cook, whisking constantly, about 1 minute, or until sauce is thickened. Remove cloves and reserve for garnish, if desired.

10 Divide pork chops among 4 dinner plates, top with sauce, and garnish each serving with a slice of orange and some cloves, if desired.

Bulgur Pilaf

3 level tablespoons unsalted butter or margarine
60 g (2 oz) slivered almonds
125 g (4 oz) bulgur
250 ml (8 fl oz) chicken stock
Small bunch parsley
125 g (4 oz) dark or golden raisins
1 level tablespoon grated orange rind

1 Line plate with double thickness of paper towels.

2 Heat butter or margarine in medium-size saucepan over medium heat. Add almonds and sauté, stirring, 2 minutes, or just until golden. With slotted spoon, transfer almonds to paper-towel-lined plate; set aside to drain.

3 Add bulgur to butter or margarine remaining in saucepan and sauté, stirring 1 minute, or just until well coated.

4 Stir in stock and bring to a boil over high heat. Reduce heat to low, cover, and simmer, undisturbed, 25 to 30 minutes, or until liquid is totaly absorbed.

5 Wash parsley and dry with paper towels. Trim stem ends and discard. Mince enough parsley to measure 15 g (1/2 oz); reserve remainder for another use.

6 Add almonds, parsley, raisins, and orange rind to bulgur and toss gently to combine. Turn into ovenproof bowl and keep warm in 200°C (400°F or Mark 6) oven until ready to serve.

Peas with Mint

Small bunch fresh mint, or 2 teaspoons dried
2 small cloves garlic
1 level tablespoon unsalted butter or margarine
500 g (16 oz) bag frozen peas, thawed
1/4 teaspoon salt
Pinch of freshly ground pepper

1 Preheat oven to 200°C (400°F or Mark 6).

2 Wash fresh mint, if using, and pat dry with paper towels. Mince enough mint leaves to measure 15 g (1/2 oz); set aside. Reserve remainder for another use.

3 Peel and mince enough garlic to measure 2 teaspoons.

4 Heat butter or margarine in medium-size skillet over medium heat. Add garlic and sauté, stirring occasionally, 1 minute, or until transparent; do *not* brown.

5 Add peas, mint, salt, and pepper to pan, and cook, stirring gently, about 5 minutes, or until heated through.

6 Turn peas into heatproof bowl, cover loosely with foil, and keep warm in oven until ready to serve.

Honey-Lime Chicken Breasts
Corn with Peppers and Onion
Cheddar Drop Biscuits

Sit your family down to a tempting meal of chicken breasts with honey-lime sauce, corn with diced peppers and onion, and warm Cheddar cheese biscuits. Serve extra biscuits in a napkin-lined basket.

Flattening the chicken breasts before cooking ensures that they cook through quickly. Pound them from the centre outward, so each breast is of even thickness.

Start-to-Finish Steps

One hour ahead: Set out corn to thaw.

1. Follow biscuits recipe steps 1 to 7.
2. Follow corn recipe steps 1 and 2.
3. Follow biscuits recipe step 8, reduce oven temperature to 200°C (400°F or Mark 6), and follow corn recipe steps 3 to 7.
4. Follow chicken recipe steps 1 to 6.
5. While chicken cooks, follow biscuits recipe step 9.
6. Follow chicken recipe steps 7 to 10, corn recipe step 8, and serve with biscuits.

Honey-Lime Chicken Breasts

2 large limes
30 g (1 oz) plain flour, approximately
2 whole boneless, skinless chicken breasts, halved (about 500 g (1 lb) total weight)
2 level tablespoons unsalted butter
2 tablespoons olive or vegetable oil
175 ml (6 fl oz) chicken stock
150 ml (5 fl oz) honey
$^1/_4$ teaspoon salt
Pinch of Cayenne pepper

1. Wash one lime and dry with paper towel. Using grater or zester, grate rind from lime, avoiding white pith as much as possible; set aside. Squeeze enough juice from peeled lime plus second lime to measure 30 g (1 oz); set juice aside.
2. Place flour in pie plate; set aside.
3. Wash and dry chicken. Place each chicken breast half between two sheets of waxed paper and pound to $2^1/_2$ mm ($^1/_8$ inch) thickness with meat mallet or rolling pin.
4. Heat butter and oil in large heavy-gauge skillet over medium-high heat.
5. Working quickly, dredge each breast half in flour, gently shake off excess, and add to hot fat in skillet. Sauté breasts 3 minutes per side, or until browned.
6. Add stock to skillet and bring to a boil. Reduce heat

to low, cover, and simmer 3 to 5 minutes, or until breasts are fork-tender.

7 Transfer chicken breasts to heatproof platter, cover loosely with foil, and keep warm in 200°C (400°F or Mark 6) oven.

8 For sauce, add honey, grated rind, salt, and Cayenne pepper to liquid in skillet and stir until blended. Increase heat to high, bring to a rapid boil, and boil 5 to 7 minutes, or until sauce is reduced and slightly thickened.

9 Add lime juice to sauce and stir until blended; remove skillet from heat.

10 Divide chicken breasts among 4 dinner plates and top with equal portions of sauce.

Corn with Peppers and Onion

Medium-size red bell pepper
Medium-size green bell pepper
Small onion
2 tablespoons olive or vegetable oil
Small bunch parsley
1 lemon (if using avocado)
Small avocado (optional)
300 g (10 oz) package frozen corn kernels, thawed
    and drained
$^1/_4$ teaspoon salt

1 Wash and dry bell peppers. Halve, core, and seed. Coarsely chop enough peppers to measure 175 g (6 oz) total.

2 Peel onion and cut crosswise into thin slices.

3 Heat oil in medium-size heavy-gauge skillet over medium heat. Add peppers and onion, and sauté, stirring occasionally, about 10 minutes, or until tender but not browned.

4 Meanwhile, wash and dry parsley. Trim stem ends and discard. Chop enough parsley to measure 15 g ($^1/_2$ oz); set aside. Reserve remainder for another use.

5 If using avocado, squeeze enough lemon juice to measure 2 tablespoons; set aside.

6 Halve avocado lengthwise, cutting around and under pit. Twist halves in opposite directions to separate. Remove and discard pit. Peel avocado, cut into 1 cm ($^1/_2$ inch) dice, and place in small bowl. Sprinkle with lemon juice to prevent discolouration and toss gently until evenly coated.

7 Add corn and salt to vegetables into medium-size heatproof bowl, cover with foil, and keep warm in 200°C (400°F or Mark 6) oven.

8 Just before serving, fold in parsley and avocado. Divide among 4 dinner plates and serve.

Cheddar Drop Biscuits

125 g ($^1/_4$ lb) Cheddar cheese
4 level tablespoons unsalted butter, well chilled
250 g (8 oz) plain flour
2 teaspoons baking powder
$^1/_4$ teaspoon baking soda
$^1/_2$ teaspoon salt
$^1/_2$ teaspoon dried thyme
250 ml (8 fl oz) buttermilk

1 Preheat oven to 220°C (450°F or Mark 8).

2 Using grater, shred enough Cheddar to measure 100 g (3 oz); set aside.

3 Cut butter into quarters; set aside.

4 Combine flour, baking powder, baking soda, salt, and thyme in medium-size bowl and stir with fork to blend.

5 Using pastry blender or 2 knives, cut in butter until mixture resembles coarse cornmeal.

6 With wooden spoon, stir in buttermilk and two thirds of the shredded Cheddar, and beat vigorously 30 seconds.

7 Drop batter by heaping tablespoonfuls at least 5 cm (2 inches) apart onto ungreased baking sheet, making 10 to 12 biscuits. Sprinkle each biscuit with remaining Cheddar and bake 8 to 10 minutes, or until puffed and golden.

8 Transfer biscuits to wire cooling racks.

9 A few minutes before serving, wrap biscuits loosely in foil and place in oven to warm, if desired.

Nina Simonds

Menu 1
(*Right*)
Turkey, Pepper, and Mushroom Kebabs
Chilled Rice and Vegetable Salad

Nina Simonds, who has earned her culinary reputation as an expert chef and teacher of Chinese cooking, can easily make the transition to other cuisines as well. She finds this a particularly valuable skill when planning family menus. 'Serving food from a number of different countries,' she says, 'is an ideal way to introduce children to unusual ingredients and dishes.' The three menus she offers here demonstrate her eclectic approach to home cooking.

Poultry is one of Nina Simond's favourite meats because it is generally lean, high in protein, and adaptable to a variety of seasonings and cooking methods. For Menu 1, a Mediterranean-style meal, she selects turkey breast meat, which she cubes and then marinates on skewers with mushrooms and peppers for kebabs. With the kebabs she provides a colourful rice and vegetable salad.

Chicken drumsticks – ideal finger food for children – are the focus of her country-French Menu 2. She serves the chicken with two tempting vegetable dishes: broccoli sautéed with bacon, and carrots coated with a honey-lemon glaze.

Chinese flavours mingle in Menu 3, in which poussins are marinated in a *hoisin*-based sauce for the entrée. Snow peas and almonds stir-fried with sesame oil, and a salad of bean sprouts and red pepper strips in a soy sauce and rice vinegar dressing are the Oriental accompaniments.

Grill cubed turkey, mushrooms, and green peppers on fanciful skewers for a delicious family meal. The bold linens and dinnerware pick up the colours of the rice and vegetable salad.

Turkey, Pepper, and Mushroom Kebabs
Chilled Rice and Vegetable Salad

Packaged turkey breast is readily available fresh or frozen at most supermarkets. Even though turkey breast is fairly tender, marinating it tenderizes the meat further and adds flavour. Heating the marinade helps it to penetrate the meat cubes more rapidly.

A chilled rice and vegetable salad sparked with a pungent dressing is a flavourful complement to the turkey kebabs. Be sure to chill the cooked rice before assembling the salad so that the grains do not stick together.

If you are serving the kebabs to young children, you may want to remove the turkey, peppers, and mushrooms from the skewers once cooked.

Start-to-Finish Steps

1 Follow rice salad recipe step 1 and kebabs recipe step 1.
2 Follow rice salad recipe step 2.
3 While rice simmers, wash parsley, and fresh basil and oregano if using; pat dry with paper towels. Trim stem ends and discard. Chop enough parsley to measure 2 tablespoons for rice salad recipe. Set aside 4 basil sprigs for garnish, if using, and chop enough basil leaves to measure 1 teaspoon for kebabs recipe. Chop enough oregano to measure 2 teaspoons for kebabs recipe. Reserve remaining herbs for another use.
4 Follow kebabs recipe steps 2 to 4.
5 Follow rice salad recipe step 3 and kebabs recipe steps 5 to 9.
6 Follow rice salad recipe steps 4 to 6 and kebabs recipe step 10.
7 Follow rice salad recipe steps 7 to 9.
8 Follow kebabs recipe steps 11 to 14 and serve with rice salad.

Turkey, Pepper, and Mushroom Kebabs

Marinade:
2 cloves garlic
250 ml (8 fl oz) olive oil
125 ml (4 fl oz) dry red wine
2 tablespoons red wine vinegar
1 teaspoon salt
2 teaspoons chopped fresh oregano, or 1 teaspoon dried
1 teaspoon chopped fresh basil, or 1/2 teaspoon dried
1/2 teaspoon freshly ground black pepper
250 g (1/2 lb) button mushrooms
2 medium-size green bell peppers (about 250 g (1/2 lb) total weight)
1/2 boneless turkey breast (about 750 g (1 1/2 lb))

Garnishes (optional):
1 lemon
4 sprigs fresh basil

1 If using bamboo skewers, place 8 in a 23 by 30 cm (9 by 12 inch) shallow flameproof glass or ceramic baking dish, add enough cold water to cover, and set aside to soak.
2 Bruise garlic under flat blade of chef's knife; remove and discard peels.
3 In small non-aluminium saucepan, combine marinade ingredients and bring to a boil over high heat. Reduce heat to medium and simmer 5 minutes.
4 Remove marinade from heat and set aside to cool.
5 Wipe mushrooms clean with damp paper towels. Trim stem ends and discard. Set aside.
6 Wash peppers and dry with paper towels. Halve, core, and seed peppers. Cut into 3 1/2 cm (1 1/2 inch) squares; set aside.
7 Remove and discard skin and any cartilage from turkey breast. Cut breast into 3 1/2 cm (1 1/2 inch) cubes; set aside.
8 Remove skewers from water, if necessary, and dry baking dish. Thread turkey cubes, green pepper squares, and mushrooms alternately on 8 skewers and place kebabs in baking dish.
9 Pour marinade over kebabs and turn to coat. Set aside to marinate at room temperature at least 15 minutes, turning every 5 minutes.

10 Preheat grill.

11 Place baking dish with kebabs and marinade 8 to 10 cm (3 to 4 inches) from heating element and grill kebabs 12 to 15 minutes on one side, basting if desired, until turkey is brown.

12 Turn skewers and grill another 12 to 15 minutes, basting if desired.

13 Wash lemon, if using, and dry with paper towel. Cut four 5 mm ($^1/_4$ inch) thick slices; set aside.

14 Place 2 skewers on each of 4 dinner plates and garnish each serving with a slice of lemon and a sprig of basil, if desired.

Chilled Rice and Vegetable Salad

250 g (8 oz) long-grain rice
2 medium-size tomatoes (about 500 g (1 lb) total weight)
2 ripe avocados
Medium-size red onion
2 tablespoons minced parsley

Dressing:
4 tablespoons olive oil
4 tablespoons safflower or corn oil
4 tablespoons red wine vinegar
1 teaspoon Dijon mustard
1$^1/_4$ teaspoons salt
$^1/_4$ teaspoon freshly ground black pepper

1 Bring 750 ml (1$^1/_2$ pts) water to a boil in medium-size heavy-gauge saucepan over high heat.

2 Stir rice into boiling water. Cover, reduce heat to medium-low, and simmer gently, undisturbed, 18 to 20 minutes, or until water is completely absorbed.

3 Fluff rice with fork and transfer to jelly-roll pan. Spread out rice evenly in pan, cover with plastic wrap, and place in freezer to chill.

4 Wash tomatoes and dry with paper towels. Core and halve each tomato crosswise. Gently squeeze each half to remove seeds. Cut tomatoes into 1 cm ($^1/_2$ inch) cubes; set aside.

5 Halve each avocado lengthwise, cutting around pit. Twist halves in opposite directions to separate; remove and discard pits. Peel avocados and cut into 1 cm ($^1/_2$ inch) cubes; set aside.

6 Halve, peel, and coarsely dice enough onion to measure 125 g (4 oz); set aside.

7 Combine chilled rice, tomatoes, avocados, onion, and parsley in large bowl and toss gently to combine.

8 Combine dresing ingredients in small non-aluminium bowl and whisk vigorously until well blended.

9 Pour dressing over rice salad and toss gently until evenly coated. Cover with plastic wrap and refrigerate until ready to serve.

Added touch
Choose slightly underripe bananas for this elegant fruit dessert. If the bananas are overripe, they will be too pulpy after baking and will lose their shape.

Baked Bananas with Shaved Chocolate

4 level tablespoons unsalted butter
1 lemon
4 slightly underripe bananas
125 g (4 oz) granulated sugar
125 ml (4 fl oz) Grand Marnier or other orange-flavoured liqueur (optional)
4 level tablespoons sweet dark chocolate shavings

1 Preheat oven 200°C (400°F or Mark 6).

2 In small saucepan, melt butter over low heat.

3 Meanwhile, squeeze enough lemon juice to measure 2 tablespoons; set aside.

4 Cut four 30 cm (12 inch) square sheets of foil and brush dull side of each generously with melted butter.

5 Peel and halve bananas lengthwise. Place a pair of halves, cut-sides-up, in centre of 1 foil square. Sprinkle bananas with lemon juice, sugar, and Grand Marnier if using, and reassemble halves. Turn bananas on diagonal in centre of foil squares, fold foil to form triangle, and seal edges.

6 Transfer foil packets to baking sheet and bake bananas 8 to 10 minutes, or until fragrant.

7 Transfer packets to dessert plates and cut foil open. Sprinkle each serving with shaved chocolate and serve.

Chicken Drumsticks with Tarragon-Shallot Butter
Sautéed Broccoli with Bacon and Onion
Glazed Carrots

For a casual buffet, offer chicken drumsticks arranged around sautéed broccoli, and a second platter of glazed carrots.

Choose meaty drumsticks so that two per person will be a substantial entrée. The drumsticks are enriched with tarragon, shallots, and butter stuffed into a pocket made by slitting one side of the drumstick. As the chicken cooks, the butter and seasonings permeate and moisten the meat.

Start-to-Finish Steps

1 Prepare herbs for drumsticks and carrot recipes. Reserve remaining herbs for another use.
2 Follow drumsticks recipe steps 1 to 5.
3 While drumsticks are browning, follow broccoli recipe steps 1 to 3.
4 Follow drumsticks recipe step 6.
5 Follow carrots recipe steps 1 to 4.
6 While carrots simmer, follow broccoli recipe steps 4 to 7.
7 Follow carrots recipe step 5, drumsticks recipe step 7, and broccoli recipe step 8.
8 Follow drumsticks recipe steps 8 to 12, carrots recipe step 6, and serve with broccoli.

Chicken Drumsticks with Tarragon-Shallot Butter

2 shallots
2 level tablespoons chopped fresh tarragon, or 1 tablespoon dried
1 teaspoon salt
$^1/_2$ teaspoon freshly ground black pepper
4 level tablespoons unsalted butter
8 meaty chicken drumsticks (about 1 kg (2 lbs) total weight)
3 tablespoons safflower or corn oil
125 ml (4 fl oz) dry white wine
Large egg
175 ml (6 fl oz) heavy cream
1 level tablespoon chopped fresh parsley for garnish

1 Peel and mince enough shallots to measure 1 level tablespoon.
2 Combine shallots, tarragon, $^1/_2$ teaspoon salt, and $^1/_4$ teaspoon pepper in small bowl and blend with fork.
3 Cut butter into 8 equal pieces.
4 Rinse drumsticks under cold running water and dry with paper towels. Cut a 5 cm (2 inch) long by 1 cm ($^1/_2$ inch) deep slit down the flat side of each drumstick, parallel to the bone. Using tip of paring knife, pry slit apart to make small pocket. Stuff each pocket with some of herb mixture, then push in piece of butter. Rinse and dry bowl.

5 Heat oil in large heavy-gauge skillet or sauté pan until very hot but not smoking. Add drumsticks to skillet, pocket-sides-up, and fry over high heat, turning once or twice, about 10 minutes, or until golden brown.
6 Add wine and cover pan. Reduce heat to low and simmer 20 to 25 minutes, or until chicken is tender and juices run clear when drumsticks are pierced with tip of knife.
7 Using tongs, transfer drumsticks, pocket-sides-down, to heatproof serving platter, cover loosely with foil, and keep warm in 200°C (400°F or Mark 6) oven until ready to serve.
8 Raise heat under skillet to medium-high and reduce pan juices 3 to 4 minutes, or until thick enough to coat the back of a spoon.
9 Meanwhile, separate egg, placing yolk in small bowl and reserving white for another use.
10 Add cream to yolk and whisk until blended.
11 Whisking continuously, slowly add about 60 ml (2 fl oz) of the reduced pan juices to cream mixture and whisk until well blended. Reduce heat under skillet to medium-low and, whisking continuously, gradually add sauce to pan. Simmer sauce 1 to 2 minutes, or until thickened. Do *not* allow sauce to boil.
12 Whisk in remaining $^1/_2$ teaspoon salt and $^1/_4$ teaspoon pepper; taste and adjust seasoning. Pour half of the sauce over drumsticks and sprinkle with chopped parsley. Serve remaining sauce separately.

Sautéed Broccoli with Bacon and Onion

1 bunch broccoli (about 625 g (1$^1/_4$ lbs))
Medium-size yellow onion
125 g ($^1/_4$ lb) sliced bacon
125 ml (4 fl oz) chicken stock
$^1/_2$ teaspoon salt
$^1/_4$ teaspoon freshly ground black pepper

1 Wash and dry broccoli. Cut tops into florets. Trim stem ends, peel stems, if desired, and cut stems crosswise on diagonal into 2$^1/_2$ cm (1 inch) pieces; set aside.
2 Halve, peel, and mince enough onion to measure 125 g (4 oz); set aside.
3 Coarsely chop bacon.
4 In medium-size heavy-gauge skillet or sauté pan, cook bacon over medium heat, stirring constantly, 2 to 3 minutes.

5 Add onion and sauté, stirring constantly, 2 to 3 minutes, or until onion is soft and transparent and bacon is cooked.
6 Add broccoli and cook over high heat, tossing gently, 1 minute.
7 Stir in chicken stock, salt, and pepper. Partially cover pan, reduce heat to medium, and cook 3 to 5 minutes, or until broccoli is tender.
8 Transfer broccoli to heatproof platter, cover with foil, and keep warm in 200°C (400°F or Mark 6) oven until ready to serve.

Glazed Carrots

4 large carrots (about 500 g (1 lb) total weight), or 500 g (1 lb) baby carrots
1 lemon
2 level tablespoons unsalted butter
1 tablespoon honey
1 teaspoon salt
¹/₄ teaspoon freshly ground black pepper
1 tablespoon chopped fresh parsley

1 Peel and trim carrots. If using large carrots, cut crosswise into thirds, then quarter each piece lengthwise; set carrots aside.
2 Squeeze enough lemon juice to measure 2 tablespoons; reserve remaining lemon for another use.

3 Combine carrots, lemon juice, butter, honey, 125 ml (4 fl oz) water, salt, and pepper in medium-size saucepan and bring to a boil over medium-high heat. Partially cover pan, reduce heat to medium-low, and cook gently 10 to 12 minutes, or until carrots are tender and sauce has reduced to a thick glaze.
4 Preheat oven to 200°C (400°F or Mark 6).
5 Turn carrots and glaze onto heatproof serving platter, cover loosely with foil, and keep warm in oven until ready to serve.
6 Just before serving, sprinkle carrots with parsley.

Added touch
Unlike more delicate custards, this sturdy version does not curdle easily. Take care not to overcook it, though, or its surface will dimple.

Coconut Custard

250 ml (8 fl oz) half-and-half milk and cream
125 ml (4 fl oz) heavy cream
3 large eggs
125 g (4 oz) granulated sugar
30 g (1 oz) sweetened flaked coconut
1 teaspoon vanilla extract
2 teaspoons cinnamon

1 Preheat oven to 170°C (325°F or Mark 3).
2 Combine half-and-half and cream in small non-aluminium saucepan and heat mixture over medium-low heat about 3 minutes until just scalded.
3 Meanwhile, separate 2 eggs, placing yolks in medium-size non-aluminium bowl and reserving whites for another use.
4 Add remaining whole egg and sugar to yolks, and whisk until well blended.
5 Whisking continuously, slowly add scalded cream mixture to egg mixture and whisk until blended. Stir in coconut and vanilla extract.
6 Divide mixture among 4 custard cups or 250 g (8 oz) ramekins and sprinkle each portion with ¹/₂ teaspoon cinnamon.
7 Place ramekins in large baking dish or roasting pan. Fill dish to a depth of 2¹/₂ cm (1 inch) with warm water and bake custards, uncovered, 35 to 45 minutes, or until a knife inserted in the centre comes out clean.
8 Remove custards from baking dish and set aside to cool slightly. Serve warm.

Menu 3

Poussins Oriental-Style
Stir-Fried Snow Peas with Almonds
Sweet Red Pepper and Bean Sprout Salad

The poussins are marinated in and basted with a robust sauce containing Chinese *hoisin* sauce, a sweet soybean-based mixture flavoured with vinegar and spices. Look for *hoisin* sauce in cans or jars at Chinese groceries or in the Oriental foods section of well-stocked supermarkets.

Start-to-Finish Steps
1 Follow poussins recipe steps 1 to 5.

2 While poussins are marinating, follow salad recipe steps 1 to 3.
3 Follow poussins recipe step 6.
4 While poussins are roasting, follow salad recipe steps 4 and 5, and snow peas recipe steps 1 and 2.
5 Follow poussins recipe steps 7 to 9.
6 Follow snow peas recipe steps 3 to 6, and poussins recipe step 10, and serve with salad.

Poussins, roasted until crispy, are accompanied by stir-fried snow peas with almonds and a sprout and red pepper salad.

Roasted Poussins Oriental-Style

2 whole 625 g to 750 g (1¼ to 1½lb) poussins

Marinade:
2 cloves garlic
60 ml (2 fl oz) hoisin sauce, if available
2 tablespoons Chinese soy sauce, or 3 tablespoons if not using hoisin sauce
1½ tablespoons ketchup, or 3 tablespoons if not using hoisin sauce
1 level tablespoon light brown sugar
1 teaspoon Oriental sesame oil, or 1½ teaspoons if not using hoisin sauce

Garnishes (optional)
8 sprigs Italian parsley
Small red bell pepper

1 Rinse poussins and dry with paper towels. Remove and discard any excess fat or cartilage from cavity and neck. Place poussins in roasting pan; set aside.
2 Bruise garlic cloves under flat blade of chef's knife; remove peel and discard. Mince garlic and place in small bowl.
3 Add hoisin sauce, if using, soy sauce, ketchup, sugar, and sesame oil, and stir until blended.
4 Pour sauce over poussins, completely coating outside and cavity of each poussin; set aside to marinate at least 10 minutes.
5 Preheat oven to 180°C (350°F or Mark 4).
6 Turn poussins breast-side-down and roast 25 minutes, basting occasionally.
7 Turn poussins breast-side-up and roast another 20 minutes, basting occasionally.
8 Meanwhile, wash parsley, if using, and pat dry with paper towels. Trim stems and discard. Set aside.
9 Wash red bell pepper, if using, and dry with paper towel. Halve, core, and seed pepper. Cut one half lengthwise into 5 mm (¼ inch) wide strips; reserve remainder for another use.
10 Remove poussins from oven and split in half with poultry shears. Transfer to 4 dinner plates and garnish each serving with parsley sprigs and bell pepper strips, if desired.

Stir-Fried Snow Peas with Almonds

250 g (½ lb) snow peas
2 tablespoons chicken stock
1 teaspoon salt
½ teaspoon granulated sugar
1½ teaspoons Oriental sesame oil
60 g (2 oz) sliced almonds

1 Trim ends and remove strings from snow peas. Place snow peas in colander, rinse under cold running water, and set aside to drain.
2 Combine chicken stock, salt, and sugar in small bowl, and stir until sugar dissolves; set aside.
3 Place large heavy-gauge skillet over medium-high heat. Add sesame oil and heat, swirling oil to coat pan, about 45 seconds, or until oil is just about to smoke. Add snow peas and stir-fry about 1 minute, or until vivid green in colour.
4 Add stock mixture to skillet and cook snow peas, tossing gently, 1 minute.
5 Add sliced almonds and toss until almonds are evenly distributed and coated with sauce.
6 Divide snow peas and almonds among dinner plates and serve immediately.

Sweet Red Pepper and Bean Sprout Salad

2 medium-size red bell peppers
250 g (½ lb) bean sprouts
2 tablespoons Chinese soy sauce
1½ tablespoons Chinese rice vinegar
1½ teaspoons Oriental sesame oil
1½ teaspoons granulated sugar
1 teaspoon salt

1   Bring 1¼ ltrs (2 pts) water to a boil in small saucepan over high heat.
2   Meanwhile, halve, core, and seed red bell peppers. Cut peppers lengthwise into 2½ mm (⅛ inch) wide strips. You should have about 125 g (4 oz) strips. Plunge pepper strips into boiling water and cook about 15 seconds. Turn into colander and immediately refresh under cold running water. Drain thoroughly and dry with paper towels. Place red pepper strips in medium-size bowl; set aside.

3   Place bean sprouts in colander and rinse gently under cold running water. Drain thoroughly and dry with paper towels. Add to bowl with pepper strips.
4   For dressing, combine soy sauce, rice vinegar, sesame oil, sugar, and salt in small bowl and stir until sugar dissolves.
5   Pour dressing over bean sprouts and peppers, and toss gently until evenly coated. Cover with plastic wrap and set aside until ready to serve.

Added touch
These poached pears are infused with the delicate tang of fresh ginger. Serve them with sugar cookies.

Poached Pears with Vanilla Ice Cream

250 g (8 oz) granulated sugar
2 cinnamon sticks
Six 2½ mm (⅛ inch) thick slices fresh ginger (about 15 g (½ oz))
1 lemon
4 slightly underripe medium-size Anjou or Bosc pears
3 slices candied ginger
500 ml (1 pt) vanilla ice cream

1   Combine sugar, 500 ml (1 pt) water, cinnamon sticks, and ginger in medium-size sauté pan and bring to a boil over medium-high heat, stirring constantly to dissolve sugar. Cook about 5 to 7 minutes, or until sugar has dissolved completely.
2   Meanwhile, wash lemon and dry with paper towel. Using sharp paring knife or zester, cut four 2½ cm (1 inch) long strips of rind; set aside. Halve lemon and squeeze juice from both halves.
3   Using vegetable peeler or sharp paring knife, peel pears. Halve each pear lengthwise; remove and discard cores. Place pear halves on large plate and sprinkle with lemon juice to prevent discolouration.
4   Add pear halves to syrup and return liquid to a boil. Reduce heat to low and poach pears, turning occasionally, about 15 minutes, or until tender when pierced with tip of knife.
5   Meanwhile, cut candied ginger and lemon rind into fine julienne strips.
6   Using slotted spoon, transfer poached pear halves to 4 dessert bowls and set aside.
7   Remove cinnamon sticks and ginger from poaching liquid. Add candied ginger and lemon rind, raise heat to high, and reduce liquid for about 15 to 20 minutes, or until thick and syrupy.
8   Spoon syrup over pears, cover with plastic wrap, and refrigerate at least 2 hours, or until chilled.
9   Just before serving, top each serving with a scoop of vanilla ice cream.

Marianne Langan

Menu 1
(*Left*)
Crispy Fried Chicken
New Potato Salad
Bacon-Corn Muffins

Marianne Langan loves to prepare meals for her family. 'I became a creative cook,' she says, 'to make eating fun for them.' Their favourite meal? Fried chicken. In Menu 1, she coats chicken pieces with beer-based batter and then pan-fries them until they are crisp and golden – a variation on the standard deep-fry recipe, which, in fact, originated in Austria, not in the American South. Other recipes for this family meal include an herbed potato salad and cornmeal muffins.

Menu 2, another Langan family favourite, also has foreign roots. This Italian meal begins with a bountiful antipasto platter of vegetables and salami to which everyone helps themselves. The antipasto is followed by chicken and vegetables in tomato sauce on a bed of *capellini* pasta, and a tossed salad with Parmesan cheese dressing.

Menu 3 is decidedly American. The buffalo chicken legs are the cooks adaption of a chicken-wing recipe that originated in Buffalo, New York, in the mid-1960s. The deep-fried drumsticks are brushed with hot sauce and accompanied by a bowl of blue cheese with crudités to cool the palate. A filling casserole of baked ham, cheese, tomato, and bread, an American classic, can be served with or after the chicken legs.

For a hearty dinner, serve crisp batter-dipped chicken pieces with potato salad and buttered cornmeal muffins. Glasses of iced tea go well with this meal.

Crispy Fried Chicken
New Potato Salad
Bacon-Corn Muffins

A simple beer batter provides the flavourful coating for the pan-fried chicken. For the best results when frying chicken, select a skillet wide enough to hold all the pieces comfortably without overlapping. If the pan is crowded, the moisture from the chicken will not evaporate, and it will stew rather than brown. If necessary, fry the chicken pieces in several batches.

Select new red potatoes for the salad: They are best for boiling because they are low in starch and hold their shape well. The skins are so thin and tender that the potatoes do not need peeling. For an interesting variation, omit the celery seeds and add 2 tablespoons of fresh snipped dill instead.

Start-to-Finish Steps

One hour ahead: Bring 3 eggs to room temperature.

1   Wash parsley and pat dry with paper towels. Trim ends and discard set aside 4 sprigs, if using for garnish for chicken recipe; chop enough parsley to measure 2 tablespoons for potato salad recipe; reserve remainder for another use.
2   Follow potato salad recipe steps 1 to 6.
3   Follow chicken recipe steps 1 to 7.
4   While chicken is frying, follow potato salad recipe steps 7 to 10 and muffins recipe steps 1 and 2.
5   Turn chicken if you haven't already, and follow muffins recipe steps 3 to 9.
6   While muffins are baking, follow chicken recipe steps 8 and 9.
7   Follow potato salad recipe steps 11 and 12.
8   Follow chicken recipe step 10 and muffins recipe step 10.
9   Follow chicken recipe step 11 and serve with potato salad and muffins.

Crispy Fried Chicken

Small clove garlic
100 g (3 oz) unsifted plain flour
$1/4$ teaspoon baking powder
$1/2$ teaspoon salt
$1/4$ teaspoon paprika
100 ml (3 fl oz) beer
1 egg, at room temperature
1 litre (1 $3/4$ pts) vegetable oil
1 $3/4$ kg (3 $1/2$ lb) frying chicken, cut into pieces, or
       1 $3/4$ kg (3 $1/2$ lb) chicken parts
1 lemon for garnish (optional)
4 parsley sprigs for garnish (optional)

1   Peel and mince garlic.
2   Combine garlic, flour, baking powder, salt, and paprika in large bowl and stir with fork to combine.
3   Combine beer, egg, and 1 tablespoon oil in small bowl and beat lightly with fork until well blended. Add beer mixture to dry ingredients and stir with fork until blended.
4   Heat remaining oil in very large, deep heavy-gauge skillet over medium-high heat until deep fat thermometer registers 190°C (375°F), or until a small cube of bread dropped in oil rises to the surface surrounded by bubbles.
5   Meanwhile, wash chicken under cold running water and dry thoroughly with paper towels; set aside.
6   Dip chicken in beer batter, several pieces at a time, and turn to coat evenly. Using tongs, transfer chicken pieces to skillet, allowing excess batter to drip off before carefully lowering chicken into hot oil. Fry 2 minutes on each side.
7   Turn chicken and fry 30 minutes, turning after 15 minutes.
8   If using lemon, wash and dry with paper towel. Cut four 5 mm ($1/4$ inch) slices from centre of lemon and set aside.
9   Line platter with double thickness of paper towels.
10 Using tongs, transfer chicken to paper-towel-lined platter to drain.
11 Divide chicken pieces among dinner plates and garnish each serving with 1 lemon slice and a parsley sprig, if desired.

New Potato Salad

750 g (1½ lbs) small new red potatoes
1 teaspoon salt
1 egg, at room temperature
Small bunch scallions
2 stalks celery
2 level tablespoons chopped parsley

Dressing:
175 g (6 oz) mayonnaise
2 tablespoons red wine vinegar
1½ teaspoons prepared mustard
¼ teaspoon celery seeds
½ teaspoon salt
Pinch of freshly ground pepper

1 Scrub potatoes under cold running water and rinse. Place potatoes in large saucepan, add salt, and enough cold water to cover, and bring to a boil over high heat. Reduce heat to medium and boil potatoes, partially covered, 10 minutes.
2 Place egg in small saucepan with enough cold water to cover and bring to a boil over medium-high heat. Cover pan, remove from heat, and set aside undisturbed 15 minutes.
3 Meanwhile, wash scallions and dry with paper towels; trim ends and discard. Cut enough scallions crosswise into 5 mm (¼ inch) pieces to measure 100 g (3 oz); set aside. Reserve remaining scallions for another use.
4 Wash celery and dry with paper towel; trim ends and discard. Cut enough celery crosswise into 5 mm (¼ inch) pieces to measure 100 g (3 oz); set aside.
5 Turn potatoes into colander and set aside to cool.
6 Drain egg and refill pan with cold water; set aside to cool.

7 When egg is cool enough to handle, peel and discard shell. Place egg in small bowl, cover with plastic wrap, and refrigerate.
8 For dressing, combine mayonnaise, vinegar, mustard, celery seeds, salt, and pepper in small bowl, and beat with fork until well blended; set aside.
9 Dry potatoes with paper towels and cut crosswise into 5 mm (¼ inch) thick slices.
10 In large bowl, combine potatoes, scallions, celery, and parsley, and toss gently to combine. Add dressing and toss until evenly coated. Cover with plastic wrap and refrigerate until ready to serve.
11 Cut egg crosswise into 2½ mm (⅛ inch) thick slices.
12 Divide potato salad among 4 dinner plates and top each serving with a few egg slices.

Bacon-Corn Muffins

4 slices bacon (125 g (4 oz) approximately
125 g (4 oz) yellow cornmeal
125 g (4 oz) plain flour
2 level tablespoons granulated sugar
1 level tablespoon baking powder
¾ teaspoon salt
250 ml (8 fl oz) milk
1 egg, at room temperature
125 g (4 oz) unsalted butter (optional)

1 Preheat oven to 220°C (425°F or Mark 7).
2 Line plate with double thickness of paper towels; set aside.
3 In medium-size skillet, cook bacon over medium-high heat, turning to cook evenly, 3 to 4 minutes, or until crisp.
4 With tongs, transfer bacon to paper-towel-lined plate to drain; reserve drippings in skillet. Crumble bacon; set aside.
5 Grease 12-cup muffin pan; set aside.
6 In large bowl, combine cornmeal, flour, sugar, baking powder, and salt, and stir with fork to combine; set aside.
7 In small bowl, combine milk, egg, and 3 tablespoons bacon drippings, and whisk until blended.
8 Add milk mixture to dry ingredients all at once. Add crumbled bacon and stir with fork just until moistened.
9 Spoon batter into prepared muffin pan, filling each cup two-thirds full, and bake 15 minutes, or until muffins are puffed and golden.
10 Turn muffins into napkin-lined basket and serve hot, with butter if desired.

Antipasto
Chicken and Vegetables in Tomato Sauce with Capellini
Tossed Salad with Parmesan Dressing

An antipasto (meaning literally 'before the food') is a customary offering at Italian meals. Intended to whet the appetite, an antipasto platter may include a wide sampling of ingredients, as this recipe shows.

Start-to-Finish Steps

One hour ahead: Set out artichokes to thaw for antipasto recipe.

1 Prepare all greens, herbs, and garlic for all recipes.
2 Follow antipasto recipe steps 1 to 8.
3 Follow salad recipe steps 1 to 6.
4 Follow chicken recipe steps 1 to 7.

This colourful Italian dinner includes a meat and vegetable antipasto with watercress dressing, a main course of chicken, vegetables, and pasta, and a colourful tossed salad.

5 Follow salad recipe steps 7 and 8.
6 Follow chicken recipe step 8 and salad recipe step 9.
7 Follow chicken recipe steps 9 and 10.
8 Follow antipasto recipe step 9 and serve as first course.
9 Follow chicken recipe steps 11 and 12.
10 Follow salad recipe step 10, chicken recipe step 13, and serve.

Antipasto

Salt
125 g (¼ lb) fresh green beans
250 g (8 oz) jar fava beans

Small red bell pepper
Small cucumber
300 g (10 oz) package frozen artichoke hearts, thawed
30 g (1 oz) pimiento-stuffed green olives
8 leaves red leaf lettuce
60 to 125 g (2 to 4 oz) thinly sliced Italian salami

Dressing:
125 ml (4 fl oz) olive oil
2 tablespoons balsamic or red wine vinegar
30 g (1 oz) watercress leaves
Small clove garlic, crushed and peeled
Freshly ground pepper

1 Bring 1¼ ltrs (2 pts) lightly salted water to a boil in medium-size saucepan over high heat.
2 While water is heating, trim ends of green beans. Plunge beans into boiling water and cook 3 minutes.
3 Rinse fava beans in strainer; set aside to drain.
4 Refresh green beans in colander under cold water; drain.
5 Wash and dry red pepper. Halve, core, and seed pepper. Quarter each half lengthwise; set aside.
6 Wash and dry cucumber. Halve crosswise. Using fork, score one half lengthwise and then cut crosswise into 5 mm (¼ inch) thick slices. Reserve remaining half for another use.
7 Pat artichoke hearts dry with paper towels. Drain olives.
8 Line serving platter with lettuce; arrange vegetables, olives, and salami attractively on lettuce. Cover with plastic wrap and refrigerate until ready to serve.
9 In food processor or blender process dressing ingredients until smooth. Add salt and pepper to taste. Turn dressing into small jug and serve with antipasto.

Chicken and Vegetables in Tomato Sauce with Capellini

Medium-size courgette (about 250 g (½ lb))
8 medium-size mushrooms (about 175 g (6 oz))

Medium-size yellow onion
850 g (28 oz) can Italian plum tomatoes
2 whole boneless, skinless chicken breasts, halved
3 tablespoons olive oil
175 ml (6 fl oz) chicken stock
2 teaspoons minced garlic
1 level tablespoon chopped fresh basil, or ¹/₂ teaspoon
   dried
Salt and freshly ground white pepper
250 g (8 oz) dried capellini

1 Scrub, rinse, and dry courgette. Cut enough crosswise into 5 mm (¹/₄ inch) slices to measure 125 g (4 oz).

2 Wipe mushrooms clean with damp paper towels. Trim stems and discard. Cut enough mushrooms into 5 mm (¹/₄ inch) thick slices; set aside.

3 Coarsely chop enough onion to measure 125 g (4 oz).

4 Drain tomatoes, reserving juice for another use. Chop enough tomatoes to measure 625 g (1¹/₄ lbs) and set aside.

5 Preheat oven to 200°C (400°F or Mark 6).

6 Wash chicken breasts and pat dry with paper towels. Cut into 7¹/₂ cm long by 1 cm wide (3 by ¹/₂ inch) wide strips; set aside.

7 In large heavy-gauge skillet, heat 2 tablespoons oil over medium-high heat. Add chicken and sauté, stirring occasionally, 4 minutes, or until browned.

8 Add courgette, mushrooms, and onion, and sauté 2 to 3 minutes, or until vegetables are slightly softened.

9 Add tomatoes, stock, minced garlic, basil, 1 teaspoon salt, and pepper to skillet, and stir to combine. Reduce heat to medium-low, cover skillet, and simmer 15 minutes, or until chicken and vegetables are fork-tender.

10 Bring 3¹/₂ ltrs (6 pts) water, 1 tablespoon oil, and 1 level tablespoon salt to a boil in large saucepan over medium heat.

11 Place heatproof serving platter in oven to warm.

12 Add pasta to boiling water; stir to separate strands. Cook 8 to 10 minutes, or just until *al dente*. Drain.

13 Transfer pasta to warm serving platter, top with chicken and vegetables, and serve.

Tossed Salad with Parmesan Dressing

6 red radishes
Small yellow and green bell pepper
60 g (2 oz) alfalfa sprouts
8 medium-size mushrooms (about 175 g (6 oz))
Small red onion
250 g (8 oz) mixed salad greens such as romaine,
   leaf lettuce, or chicory, in any combination

Dressing:
60 g (2 oz) Parmesan cheese
¹/₂ teaspoon dried oregano
125 ml (4 fl oz) vegetable oil
125 ml (4 fl oz) balsamic or red wine vinegar
1 egg
Small clove garlic, crushed and peeled
2 level tablespoons minced fresh chives
¹/₂ teaspoon salt

1 Wash, dry, and trim radishes. Cut into thin slices.

2 Wash and dry bell peppers. Halve, core, and seed peppers. Cut lengthwise into 5 mm (¹/₄ inch) wide strips; set aside.

3 Rinse and dry sprouts; set aside.

4 Clean mushrooms with damp paper towels. Trim stems and discard. Cut mushrooms into 5 mm (¹/₄ inch) slices.

5 Peel onion and slice thinly; separate into rings.

6 Place greens in salad bowl and top with vegetables. Cover and refrigerate until ready to serve.

7 Grate enough Parmesan to measure 30 g (1 oz).

8 With rolling pin, crush oregano between 2 sheets of waxed paper.

9 Combine cheese, oregano, and remaining dressing ingredients in food processor or blender and process until smooth. Transfer to small bowl, cover, and set aside.

10 When ready to serve, whisk dressing briefly to recombine and pour over salad. Toss until evenly coated.

Buffalo Chicken Legs with Blue Cheese Sauce
Baked Ham, Cheese, and Tomato Casserole
Vegetable Sauté with Mandarin Oranges

The tomato, ham, and cheese bake is also known as a strata, or layered casserole. Stratas were probably originally devised as a way to use up stale bread. This dish is ideal for busy cooks because it tastes best when assembled several hours in advance, or even the night before, and refrigerated.

Start-to-Finish Steps

1 Halve, peel, and mince enough onion to measure 2 tablespoons for casserole recipe.
2 Follow casserole recipe steps 1 to 10.
3 While casserole is baking, follow vegetables recipe steps 1 to 6.
4 Follow chicken recipe steps 1 to 7.
5 While chicken is frying, follow vegetables recipe steps 7 to 10.
6 Follow chicken recipe steps 8 to 10, vegetables recipe step 11, and serve with casserole.

Buffalo Chicken Legs with Blue Cheese Sauce

Small bunch scallions
2 stalks celery with leafy tops
1 litre (1³/₄ pts) vegetable oil
125 ml (4 fl oz) plain low-fat yogurt
2 tablespoons milk
30 g (1 oz) crumbled blue cheese
8 small chicken legs (about 750 g (1¹/₂ lbs) total weight)
100 ml (3 fl oz) hot pepper sauce (optional)

1 Wash scallions and dry with paper towels. Trim ends and discard. Halve 4 scallions lengthwise; reserve remainder for another use.
2 Wash celery and dry with paper towels; do not trim leafy tops. Halve stalks lengthwise, then cut crosswise into 7¹/₂ to 10 cm (3 to 4 inch) pieces; set aside.

Spicy chicken legs with sautéed vegetables and orange slices and a ham, cheese, and tomato casserole make satisfying family fare.

3　In large heavy-gauge saucepan or deep fryer, heat oil until deep-fat thermometer registers 190°C (375°F), or until a cube of bread dropped in oil rises to the top surrounded by bubbles.

4　Combine yogurt, milk, and cheese in small bowl and stir until well blended; the sauce will remain somewhat lumpy. Divide among 4 small serving bowls; set aside.

5　Wash chicken and dry with paper towels.

6　Line platter with double thickness of paper towels.

7　With tongs, lower chicken legs into hot oil and fry 7 to 8 minutes, or until browned and juices run clear when chicken is pierced with tip of knife.

8　Transfer chicken to towel-lined platter to drain.

9　Brush hot pepper sauce evenly over legs, if desired.

10　Divide chicken legs, celery, and scallions among 4 dinner plates, and serve with sauce on the side.

Baked Ham, Cheese, and Tomato Casserole

1 large or 3 small ripe tomatoes
6 thin slices Jarlsberg or Swiss cheese
6 thin slices baked ham
Small clove garlic
4 level tablespoons unsalted butter or margarine, at room temperature
1 teaspoon dry mustard
30 cm (12 inch) loaf French or Italian bread, or two 15 cm (6 inch) crusty rolls
625 ml (1¼ pts) milk
3 eggs
2 level tablespoons minced onion
Salt and freshly ground pepper

1　Preheat oven to 190°C (375°F or Mark 5).

2　Butter 20 by 20 cm (8 by 8 inch) baking dish; set aside.

3　Wash tomato(es) and dry with paper towel. Core and cut into total of 12 slices; set aside.

4　Halve cheese and ham slices; set aside.

5　Peel and mince garlic; set aside.

6　Combine butter, garlic, and ½ teaspoon dry mustard in small bowl and stir until well blended; set aside.

7　Cut bread into 2½ cm (1 inch) thick slices. Spread one side of each slice with butter mixture.

8　Top buttered side of each bread slice with 1 slice each of tomato, ham, and cheese, folding ham and cheese to fit bread, and place in prepared dish, standing in 3 rows of 4 slices each.

9　In medium-size bowl, combine milk, eggs, onion, remaining dry mustard, 1 teaspoon salt, and a pinch of pepper, and whisk until blended.

10　Pour milk mixture evenly over casserole and bake 45 minutes, or until puffed and golden.

Vegetable Sauté with Mandarin Oranges

2 large carrots (about 250 g (½ lb) total weight))
Medium-size courgette (about 250 g (½ lb)
2 stalks celery
Small bunch parsley
¼ teaspoon dried tarragon
125 g (4 oz) canned mandarin orange segments
1 teaspoon salt
3 level tablespoons unsalted butter

1　Peel and trim carrots. Halve each carrot lengthwise, then cut each half crosswise into 7½ cm (3 inch) pieces. Cut each piece lengthwise into 5 mm (¼ inch) julienne; set aside.

2　Scrub courgette under cold running water; rinse, and dry with paper towel. Trim ends and discard. Halve courgette lengthwise, then cut each half crosswise into 7½ cm (3 inch) pieces. Cut lengthwise into 5 mm (¼ inch) julienne; set aside.

3　Wash celery and dry with paper towels. Trim stem ends and leafy tops, and discard. Cut each stalk crosswise into 7½ cm (3 inch) pieces, then cut each piece lengthwise into 5 mm (¼ inch) julienne; set aside.

4　Wash parsley and dry with paper towels. Trim stem ends and discard. Chop enough parsley to measure 15 g (½ oz); reserve remainder for another use.

5　Crush tarragon in mortar with pestle or place between 2 sheets of waxed paper and crush with rolling pin; set aside.

6　Drain oranges; set aside.

7　In bottom of steamer unit or saucepan large enough to accommodate collapsible steamer, bring 500 ml (1 pt) of water to a boil over medium-high heat.

8　Place vegetables in steamer. Sprinkle vegetables with salt and tarragon, cover pan, and steam 4 minutes, or to desired tenderness.

9　Meanwhile, melt butter in medium-size sauté pan over medium-low heat.

10　Add steamed vegetables to butter and toss until evenly coated. Cover pan and keep warm until ready to serve.

11　Add mandarin oranges and toss briefly. Divide vegetables and oranges among dinner plates. Sprinkle each serving with 1 level tablespoon parsley, and serve.

Meet the Cooks

Diana Sturgis

Born in Wales, Diana Sturgis taught cooking and nutrition, before moving to the USA. Her background includes recipe development and testing for a New York food company and free-lance styling.

Ann Burckhardt

Born and educated in Iowa, Ann Burckhardt began her food career as an editor. She is now the author of books on food and home furnishings.

Lucy Wing

Lucy Wing lives in New York and has worked as a home economist. She has been both a contributing editor and a food editor for various magazines. Her articles have appeared in *Family Circle* and *Cuisine*.

Jane Kirby

Jane Kirby is a registered dietician who has worked in various capacities during her food career: as a hospital dietician; a test kitchen coordinator; and an assistant food editor for *Good Housekeeping* magazine.

Nina Simonds

Nina Simonds, author of *Classic Chinese Cuisine*, has translated and edited several other books, including *Chinese Cuisine* and *Chinese Snacks*. She learned to cook in Taiwan under the direction of Chinese master chef Huang Su-Huei. She also studied for a year at La Varenne Ecole de Cuisine in Paris and is the holder of a Grande Diplome in classic French cuisine.

Marianne Langan

Home economist and food stylist Marianne Langan's food career began in the test kitchens of the Campbell Soup Company. Since 1984, she has worked as a freelance cookery writer and as a stylist for many major food companies and magazines.

A Wealth of Herbs

Increasingly, herbs are arriving in the markets fresh; the proliferation of health stores and other specialist shops has widened choice, and many cooks with gardens have taken to raising their own. Recent ethnic influences have called attention to once seemingly esoteric herbs. Coriander, for one, is at last gaining deserved popularity in Europe, although cooks in Asia and the Middle East have been using it for centuries.

Anyone wishing to dry fresh herbs can tie them loosely in a bundle and hang them upside down in a cool, dark, well-ventilated place for several weeks. When the leaves are completely dried, strip them from the stems and store them in an airtight container.

Two swifter methods of preserving herbs make use of the microwave oven and the freezer. To microwave herbs, place five or six sprigs at a time between paper towels and microwave them on high for 1 to 3 minutes until the leaves are brittle. Store the leaves loosely in airtight jars.

To freeze herbs, rinse the sprigs and pat them dry. Strip the leaves off the stems and put them into a heavy-duty plastic bag. Gently flatten the bag to force out the air, seal the bag tightly, and place it in your freezer. Use the leaves as the need arises.

Basil (also called sweet basil): This fragrant herb, with its underlying flavour of anise and hint of clove, goes particularly well with tomato.

Chervil: The small, lacy leaves of this herb have a taste akin to parsley with a touch of anise. It is good in salads and salad dressings. Chervil is popular in France where it is often an ingredient in herb mixtures, including *fines herbes*. When used in cooking, chervil should be added at the end, lest its subtle flavour be lost.

Chives: The smallest of the onions, chives grow in grassy clumps. When finely cut, the hollow leaves contribute their delicate, oniony flavour to fresh salads and raw vegetables. Chives should always be used fresh, as dried ones are virtually tasteless.

Coriander (also called cilantro): The serrated leaves of the coriander plant impart a distinctive fragrance and a flavour that is both mildly sweet and bitter. Coriander leaves should be used fresh or added at the end of cooking if their flavour is to be appreciated fully.

Dill: A sprightly herb with feathery leaves, dill enhances cucumber and many other fresh vegetables, as well as fish and shellfish. When used in cooking, dill should be added towards the end of the process to preserve its delicate flavour. Both dill seeds and dill leaves can be